First World War
and Army of Occupation
War Diary
France, Belgium and Germany

61 DIVISION
183 Infantry Brigade,
Brigade Trench Mortar Battery
2 July 1916 - 15 July 1916

WO95/3062/4

The Naval & Military Press Ltd
www.nmarchive.com
Published in association with The National Archives

Published by

The Naval & Military Press Ltd

Unit 10 Ridgewood Industrial Park,

Uckfield, East Sussex,

TN22 5QE England

Tel: +44 (0) 1825 749494

www.naval-military-press.com

www.nmarchive.com

This diary has been reprinted in facsimile from the original. Any imperfections are inevitably reproduced and the quality may fall short of modern type and cartographic standards.

© **Crown Copyright**
Images reproduced by permission of The National Archives, London, England, 2015.

Contents

Document type	Place/Title	Date From	Date To
War Diary	Fauquissart Sector	16/07/1916	02/08/1916
Heading	183rd Inf Bde War Diary of 183 Light Trench Mortar Battery August 1st-31st 1916 Vol 4		
War Diary	Fauquissart Sector	01/08/1916	18/08/1916
War Diary	Heuve Chapelle Feruer du Bois	18/08/1916	25/08/1916
War Diary	Moated Grange Sector	26/08/1916	31/08/1916
Heading	183 T.M.B IV Army Routine Orders		
Miscellaneous	Routine Orders By General Sir H.S Rawlinson Bart. K.C.B K.C.V.O. Commanding Fourth Army	10/03/1917	10/03/1917
Miscellaneous	Routine Orders By General Sir H.S Rawlinson Bart. K.C.B K.C.V.O. Commanding Fourth Army	16/04/1917	16/04/1917
Miscellaneous	Routine Orders By General Sir H.S Rawlinson Bart. K.C.B K.C.V.O. Commanding Fourth Army	20/04/1917	20/04/1917
Heading	183 L.M.B 183rd Brigade Orders 5-1-17 To 9-6-17		
Operation(al) Order(s)	Brigade Routine Order by Brigadier General A.H. Spooner D.S.O. Commanding 183rd Infantry Brigade	05/01/1917	05/01/1917
Operation(al) Order(s)	Brigade Order No.132 by Brigadier General A.H. Spooner D.S.O. Commanding 183rd Infantry Brigade	23/05/1917	23/05/1917
Operation(al) Order(s)	Brigade Order No.134 by Brigadier General A.H. Spooner D.S.O. Commanding 183rd Infantry Brigade	29/05/1917	29/05/1917
Miscellaneous	Administrative Addendum To 183rd Infantry Brigade Order No.123	31/05/1917	31/05/1917
Operation(al) Order(s)	Brigade Orders by Brigadier General A.H. Spooner D.S.O. Commanding 183rd Infantry Brigade	02/06/1917	02/06/1917
Operation(al) Order(s)	Brigade Orders by Brigadier General A.H. Spooner D.S.O. Commanding 183rd Infantry Brigade	06/06/1917	06/06/1917
Operation(al) Order(s)	183rd Infantry Brigade Order No.124	08/06/1917	08/06/1917
Miscellaneous	March Table "A" Issued With 183rd Inf. Bde. Order No.124	08/06/1917	08/06/1917
Miscellaneous	Administrative Addendum To 183rd Infantry Brigade Order No.124	08/06/1917	08/06/1917
Operation(al) Order(s)	Brigade Orders by Brigadier General A.H. Spooner D.S.O. Commanding 183rd Infantry Brigade	09/06/1917	09/06/1917
Heading	183 L.M.B 61st Divisional Orders February 1917		
Miscellaneous	Divisional Routine Orders By Major-General Colon Mackenzie C.B. Commanding 61st Division	25/02/1917	25/02/1917
Miscellaneous	Divisional Routine Orders By Major-General Colen Mackenzie C.B. Commanding 61st Division	28/02/1917	28/02/1917
Heading	183 L.M.B 61st Divisional Orders April 1917		
Miscellaneous	Divisional Routine Orders By Major-General Colin Mackenzie C.B. Commanding 61st Division	13/04/1917	13/04/1917
Miscellaneous	Divisional Routine Orders By Major-General Colin Mackenzie C.B. Commanding 61st Division	20/04/1917	20/04/1917
Miscellaneous	Divisional Routine Orders By Major-General Colin Mackenzie C.B. Commanding 61st Division	23/04/1917	23/04/1917
Miscellaneous	Divisional Routine Orders By Major-General Colin Mackenzie C.B. Commanding 61st Division	24/04/1917	24/04/1917
Miscellaneous	Divisional Routine Orders By Major-General Colin Mackenzie C.B. Commanding 61st Division	25/04/1917	25/04/1917
Heading	183 L.M.B 61st Divisional Orders May 1917		

Miscellaneous	Divisional Routine Orders By Major-General Colin Mackenzie C.B. Commanding 61st Division	01/05/1917	01/05/1917
Miscellaneous	Divisional Routine Orders By Major-General Colin Mackenzie C.B. Commanding 61st Division	02/05/1917	02/05/1917
Miscellaneous	Divisional Routine Orders By Major-General Colin Mackenzie C.B. Commanding 61st Division	04/05/1917	04/05/1917
Miscellaneous	Divisional Routine Orders By Major-General Colin Mackenzie C.B. Commanding 61st Division	07/05/1917	07/05/1917
Miscellaneous	Divisional Routine Orders By Major-General Colin Mackenzie C.B. Commanding 61st Division	08/05/1917	08/05/1917
Miscellaneous	Divisional Routine Orders By Major-General Colin Mackenzie C.B. Commanding 61st Division	09/05/1917	09/05/1917
Miscellaneous	Divisional Routine Orders By Major-General Colin Mackenzie C.B. Commanding 61st Division	11/05/1917	11/05/1917
Miscellaneous	Divisional Routine Orders By Major-General Colin Mackenzie C.B. Commanding 61st Division	12/05/1917	12/05/1917
Miscellaneous	Divisional Routine Orders By Major-General Colin Mackenzie C.B. Commanding 61st Division	23/05/1917	23/05/1917
Miscellaneous	Divisional Routine Orders By Major-General Colin Mackenzie C.B. Commanding 61st Division	25/05/1917	25/05/1917
Miscellaneous	Divisional Routine Orders By Major-General Colin Mackenzie C.B. Commanding 61st Division	26/05/1917	26/05/1917
Miscellaneous	Extracts From VI Corps Routine Orders Republished As An Addendum To 61st Divisional Routine Orders No.1159	25/05/1917	25/05/1917
Miscellaneous	Divisional Routine Orders By Major-General Colin Mackenzie C.B. Commanding 61st Division	28/05/1917	28/05/1917
Miscellaneous	Extracts from Third Army and VI Corps Routine Orders (Republished as an Addendum to 61st Divisional Routine Order No.1172	28/05/1917	28/05/1917
Miscellaneous	Divisional Routine Orders By Major-General Colin Mackenzie C.B. Commanding 61st Division	29/05/1917	29/05/1917
Heading	183 L.M.B Imprest Account Balance Sheets (Duplicate) June 1916 To June 1917 (Inclusive)		
Miscellaneous	For Use In The Field	27/06/1916	27/06/1916
Miscellaneous	For Use In The Field	31/07/1916	31/07/1916
Miscellaneous	For Use In The Field	31/08/1916	31/08/1916
Miscellaneous	For Use In The Field	30/09/1916	30/09/1916
Miscellaneous	For Use In The Field	31/10/1916	31/10/1916
Miscellaneous	For Use In The Field	30/11/1916	30/11/1916
Miscellaneous	For Use In The Field	31/12/1916	31/12/1916
Miscellaneous	For Use In The Field	31/01/1917	31/01/1917
Miscellaneous	For Use In The Field	28/02/1917	28/02/1917
Miscellaneous	For Use In The Field	31/03/1917	31/03/1917
Miscellaneous	For Use In The Field	30/04/1917	30/04/1917
Miscellaneous	For Use In The Field	31/05/1917	31/05/1917
Miscellaneous	For Use In The Field	30/06/1917	30/06/1917
Heading	WO95/3062-4		
Heading	61st Division 183rd Infy Bde Trench Mortar Bty Jly-Aug 1916		
Heading	War Diary of 183rd Light T.M. Battery From 1st July-31st July 1916 Vol 3		
War Diary	Fauquissart Sector	02/07/1916	15/07/1916

Army Form C. 2118.

WAR DIARY
or
INTELLIGENCE SUMMARY.
(Erase heading not required.)

183rd Seige Howitzer Battery

Place	Date	Hour	Summary of Events and Information	Remarks and references to Appendices
Fauquissart Sector	1916			
	July 16		Preparation for Gas attack it to be done by own troops. Cease firing as gas not sent off. At 10p. retaliated with 20 rounds at enemy's trench mortars.	
do	July 17		Quiet. Brought ammunition from front line.	
do	July 18		do	
do			do	
do	July 19	11am	Commenced firing & continued steadily till 5.30p. Fired approx. 600 rounds as points X14, X15, X19, X20. Four guns, ten under 227 rounds fired from "two under 229 rounds" each under. held in readiness to fire across to enemy's trenches with assembling infantry but were not needed.	
do		10p	Reinforced half battery to billets at Laventie	
do	July 20	11am	Registered on X14, X15, X19, X20. In evening took four guns to Dead End Post.	
do	July 21	10p	Fired 60 rounds on X14, X15, X19, X20. Half battery reing 6.30p	
do	July 22	11p	do	

Army Form C. 2118.

WAR DIARY
or
INTELLIGENCE SUMMARY.
(Erase heading not required.)

183rd Trench Mortar Battery.

Instructions regarding War Diaries and Intelligence Summaries are contained in F.S. Regs., Part II. and the Staff Manual respectively. Title pages will be prepared in manuscript.

Place	Date	Hour	Summary of Events and Information	Remarks and references to Appendices
Fauquissart	July 23	10am	Relieved 182 T.M.B. on right of Rifle Row with 4 guns. Registered these guns during the day. At night fired on X3, X5, X7, X8.	
do	July 24	1pm	Fired at night on above points.	
do	July 26	1.30am	Fired bin rounds rapid from 2 guns in each sector at each of these times on 2.30am	
			enemy parapet. Retaliation from enemy heavy.	
do	July 27	8-8.30am	Fired 50 rounds per gun from 3 guns on enemy parapet at [illeg] Th trick, in conjunction with Artillery, Heavy Howitzer Trench Mortars. Retaliation heavy & directed at Support line & RUE TILLELOY.	
do	July 28	11pm	Fired 20 rounds at pts X17 a X6. Retaliation slight.	
do	July 29	10.25pm	Fired 150 rounds from 3 guns at pts X14, X17, X19. Retaliation heavy, but no casualties.	
do	July 30	11.05pm	Commenced building battle emplacement N13b J5 2½ to command RED LAMP CORNER.	
do	Aug 2	12 midnight -12.30 AM.	Fired 20 rounds on pts N13 d 9 6½ & N13 a 6. 3. No retaliation.	

J. Thacker. Capt.
O/C 183 TMB

Vol 4

183rd Inf Bde

War Diary

– of –

183 Light Trench Mortar Battery

August 1st – 31st 1916.

Army Form C. 2118.

WAR DIARY
or
INTELLIGENCE SUMMARY.
(Erase heading not required.)

183 Trench Mortar Battery

Place	Date	Hour	Summary of Events and Information	Remarks and references to Appendices
Fauquissart Sector	1916			
	Aug 1-6		Work carried out on new battle emplacements at junction of NORTHUMBER- LAND AVENUE support line. New shell store commenced at junction of STRAND & TILLELOY. So firing, by Brigadier Orders	
	Aug 7.	7p	Provided gun in emplacement by bay 13. R.B. Fraired on N.19.6.0½. Another gun was held in readiness to go out of sally port bay 112 at N.19.6.0½ (N23.5-N23.1). Another gun was taken out by sally port bay 53, registered in an emplacement in the O.B.L. Fraired on sap N.19.a.2.1½. The fourth gun & two guns of the left section were fraired on our own front line at RED LAMP CORNER as usual. The gun by sally port 112 went out & took up its position at 9.30 p.m. As the 2/8 Worcester Raiding Party did not need my fire, I brought in the two guns that were out at 12.25 a.m. The guns fired on The above front at 1.10 a.m. in conjunction with the artillery, firing forty rounds.	
	Aug 8-18		In rest at La Gorgue. Time occupied in training, practising attack, gun drill, close order physical drill etc.	

Army Form C. 2118.

WAR DIARY
or
INTELLIGENCE SUMMARY.
(Erase heading not required.)

183 Trench Mortar Battery

Place	Date	Hour	Summary of Events and Information	Remarks and references to Appendices
Rue de Bois France	1916 Aug.18	10.30a.m	Accomplished reg with 94 T.M.B. facing of guns in two Offices in emplacements at the French end of Nigara trench & one at junction of S10.5, S10.6. Registered during day on pts. S11a 4½ 3, S11a 1 1, S10 a 5.5. S10 d 2.4.	
"	Aug.19 /16		Carried ammunition to front line. Registered 27 rounds on S11a 4.3, S11a 2½ 2, S10 d 6.6, S10 d 1.3½.	
"	Aug.20.		Fused & stacked 800 shells. At night six guns fired as follows: S10d 6.6, S10d 6½ 5, ammunition French joining this round. Also S11a 4, 1, S11a 4.3. These six guns fired 783 rounds during the night on the point. Ammunition carried by night from ST VAAST during to junction of RUE DU BOIS & PLUM ST.	
"	Aug.21/16	10.30p	Registered by day on S11c 0 8½ 0. S10 d 2 2. Six rounds. Ammunition carried by night to front line emplacements.	
"	Aug.22	10.30p	Fired 30 rounds on tgts S11a 7½ 5 o S11a 8½ 8½. Retaliation heavy on front line Hun SO.	

Army Form C. 2118.

WAR DIARY or INTELLIGENCE SUMMARY.

183 Siege French Mortar Battery

Place	Date	Hour	Summary of Events and Information	Remarks and references to Appendices
Henu Chapelle	1916			
Henu & Bailey Sector	Aug 23	9.30p	Guns laid on S.11.a.3½.2½, S.11.a.3½.2½, S.11.c.1.8, S.10.d.6½.3, S.10.d.4½.3, S.10.d.1½.2. Three guns opened a preliminary bombardment from 9.30p - 10.15p. Main bombardment from 12.30am - 2am, in conjunction with artillery raiding infantry. Retaliation heavy. 620 rounds fired.	
	Aug 25	6A	In conjunction with artillery machine T.M.s. fired on suspected machine gun emplacement in ruined building at S.11.a.8.8. 60 rounds fired.	
		10.30p	One hundred rounds fired at S.11.a.1.1, S.10.d.9.8½, S.10.d.6½.6. Retaliation slight.	
	Aug 26	10.30p	Was relieved by 94 2WB. By 2A had relieved 182 2WB in Monch Gorge Sector. 6 guns in line. Registered in evening on M36.S.5.6.7½.8½, M35.d.8½.7½, M36.c.3.7½, M36.c.3½.1½, M30.0.5.½, M30.0.4.4.	
Monchy Gorge Sector	Aug 27	9.0f	Four guns cooperated in a shoot against the following points:- S.3.6.7½.8½, M35.d.8½.7½, M36.c.1½.6½, M36.c.2½.7½. Shots observed to fall well on target. Retaliation heavy. 97 rounds fired. The enemy was observed carrying ammunition from Epinette Green to the enemy's trenches.	

WAR DIARY
or
INTELLIGENCE SUMMARY.
(Erase heading not required.)

Army Form C. 2118.

183 Trench Mortar Battery.

Instructions regarding War Diaries and Intelligence Summaries are contained in F. S. Regs., Part II. and the Staff Manual respectively. Title pages will be prepared in manuscript.

Place	Date	Hour	Summary of Events and Information	Remarks and references to Appendices
Hedauville Sector	1916 Aug 28	4.0p – 4.35pm	Three guns fired on enemy front line from M.35.a.8½ - 1½ to M.36.c.3.8 fired, Traversing right along. Three guns fired from 4.30 – 4.35 f rapid fire on M.30.c.5½.8½ @ M.30.a.9.5. The shooting was observed to be accurate – at one point duckboards were seen to rise from the enemy's trench. Rounds fired 380.	
"	Aug 29	5.15p	Guns fired on the supposed communication trenches of The BIRDCAGE @ M.30.a.4.1 @ M.30.8.5. Guns started to fire at 5.15pm, two after 10 minutes. The rate was rapid, owing to emplacements being flooded, firing was discontinued. Rounds fired 100	
"	Aug 31 – Sept 1	1.38 – 2.10am	Guns fired on same points as yesterday. Opened fire @ 1.38am – 1.58am (steady) – 1.58am – 2.10am (fairly rapid). Retaliation, heavy on front line. Rounds fired 220	

J. Shorter Capt.
O/C 183 T.M.B.

183 J. M. B.

R

IV Army Routine Orders.

Number I

No. 52.

ROUTINE ORDERS

BY

GENERAL SIR H. S. RAWLINSON, Bart.,

K.C.B., K.C.V.O., Commanding Fourth Army.

10th March, 1917.

ADJUTANT GENERAL'S BRANCH.

654—Prisoners taken by the Enemy—Caution as to Revealing Information.

General Routine Order No. 2142 is re-published:—

"A captured German Official Order shows that not only are the German General Staff at great pains to examine prisoners with a view to obtaining information of our dispositions, but also that these efforts have in several cases met with considerable success.

"The official German report of a detailed examination shows that several men disclosed information of a most valuable nature.

"It should be impressed upon all ranks that to betray one's comrades by giving information to the enemy is the act of a coward. No prisoner is compelled to state more than his name and rank, and must firmly refuse to answer any other questions. The captured document referred to above shows clearly that the enemy respects the silence of the soldier who knows his duty, and despises the weakness of the man who gives away military information."

655—Casualties.

In all cases when officers or other ranks are missing, a brief report will be made to A.H.Q. with the least possible delay.

Whenever possible this statement will be included in the Casualty Report, but, if this cannot be done, it must be stated in the Casualty Report that the report will follow.

656—Transfers to the Royal Flying Corps.

Any officers or other ranks to whom orders have been issued to report to the Royal Flying Corps Interviewing Officer, and who through the exigencies of the Service or other causes have as yet been unable to do so, will, if possible, report for the interview during the week March 12th to 17th. The Interviewing Officer will be at HEILLY on March 16th and at DOULLENS on March 17th.

657—Prevention of Chilled Feet and Frostbite.—*Continuation of A.R.O. 539.*

The opinions expressed in A.R.O. 539 have been confirmed by further experience.

The French prophylactic treatment will therefore be continued, until cases of Trench Foot cease, by the same means as before, namely:—

(a) **A Soap consisting of:**—

Soft Potash Soap	1000 parts.
Powdered Camphor	25 "
Powdered Sodium Borate	100 "

AND

(b) **A Powder consisting of:**—

Powdered Talc	1000 parts.
Camphor	25 "

The feet will first be washed in hot water with ordinary soap, and then with about a teaspoonful of soap (a). Particular care will be taken to cleanse the grooves about the toes. The chiropodist will look carefully after the nails and toes and see that the feet are carefully dried.

The feet and socks will then be dusted with powder (b).

In the trenches, the feet will be dusted with powder (b) once a day, if possible.

The process will be repeated when the troops come out of the trenches.

The quantities of the ingredients required per Division per week are, approximately:—

	lbs.
Potash Soap	300
Camphor	22
Sodium Borate	35
Talc Powder	500

658—Amendments to War Establishments—Artillery.

The following amendments to War Establishments have been approved:—

(i.) **Each Anti-Aircraft Battery.**

(*a*) One Serjeant, Army Service Corps (Mechanical Transport), to be added to the personnel attached to Headquarters.

(*b*) The number of gunners in each Section to be increased to 25 and the telephonists to four. The five extra gunners will include one cook and one orderly to take charge of billets. These will be "P.B." men or men of a category other than "A."

(ii.) **Each Workshop for Anti-Aircraft Batteries of an Army.**

One Staff Serjeant Fitter R.A. to be added.

(iii.) **6-in. Howitzer Battery (Tractor-drawn.)**

The number of Serjeants, A.S.C. (M.T.), attached, to be reduced from three to two.

(iv.) **Each Battery of R.H.A. and R.F.A.** (other than R.H.A. Batteries serving with the Cavalry Corps).

To be reduced by one trumpeter and one riding horse.

(G.H.Q. No. O.B./909, 2-3-17.)

659—Protection of Permanent Way of Light Railways.

The permanent way of light railways is not to be used as a foot or bridle path.

660—A.Fs. B. 213 and B. 213A.

A.F. B. 213 and A.F. B. 213A of all units for the week ending 17th March, 1917, will be rendered in duplicate. The duplicate copy will be forwarded direct to the Director of Supplies, General Headquarters. This duplicate copy is required for this particular week only.

661—Sale of Bread.

The French Authorities have forbidden the sale of bread by bakers or inhabitants to troops in the *communes* and *arrondissements* of DOULLENS, AMIENS, PERONNE and MONTDIDIER.

No attempts should, therefore, be made to purchase bread from bakers and inhabitants.

QUARTERMASTER GENERAL'S BRANCH.

662—Wagons Limbered G.S.—Alteration of to carry a Spare Pole.—*Reference A.R.O. 628.*

The alterations referred to in A.R.O. 628 will be made in the case of Limbered G.S. Wagons of Divisional Ammunition Columns only.

663—Spare Gun Parts—Return of to Base.

All unserviceable spare parts of Guns and Carriages will, when replaced, be returned to the Base.

It is important that such articles should not be scrapped, as it affects the output required to keep guns in action.

(63 (Q.B. 3), 1-3-17.)

664—6-in. and 4.5-in. Howitzer Shells.—*Continuation of A.R.O. 643.*

In those natures of shell which are painted black, *e.g.*, shrapnel, the longitudinal strip will be white.

(106 (Q.B. 2), 4-3-17.)

665—Correction.

In paras. (*b*) and (*c*) of A.R.O. 642, for "5 per cent." read "·5 per cent."

666—Fuzes No. 146 (Allways).

Fuzes No. 146 (Allways) for use with Stokes Mortar bombs will shortly be issued. Further issues will be packed with the bombs, and will eventually supersede the pistol head.

In using this fuze with the 3-in. Stokes bombs, a length of instantaneous fuze, with a No. 8 detonator attached, is first inserted in the cavity in the bomb, and the Allways fuze is then screwed on to the nipple of the bomb.

The instantaneous fuze used in conjunction with the No. 146 fuze must not, in any circumstances, be used with a Stokes pistol head in place of Bickford safety fuze.

The instantaneous fuze is yellow and the Bickford fuze is black.

(36/4 (Q.B. 2), 3-3-17.)

667—Trench Mortar Battery, Heavy—Equipment of.

Posts Aiming will no longer be supplied to Heavy Trench Mortar Batteries.
This item will be deleted from Mobilization Store Table A.F. G. 1098-285.

(30/18 (Q.A. 3), 5-3-17).

668—Cartridges Red (175 grains) for 3-in. Stokes Mortar.

A large number of prematures have occurred with 3-in. Stokes Mortars when using the "Red" Cartridges (175 grains).
In future, therefore, these cartridges will only be used in cases of emergency.

(36/1 (Q.B. 2), 21-2-17).

669—Live Rounds—Use of, for Lewis Guns.

I. Accidents during instruction in the use of the Lewis Gun continue to occur too often. In the majority of cases, the cause is the use of a live round either deliberately or in mistake for a dummy. The mistake is generally due to the use of dummies which are not easily distinguishable from live rounds and with which, in consequence, live rounds get mixed.

To minimise the chance of such accidents:—

(a) A live round is not to be used for drill purposes or for stripping and assembling the gun.

(b) Only the dummies provided for by this order, which cannot be mistaken for live rounds, are to be used.

(c) Before instruction, dummy rounds are to be carefully inspected.

II. There are two natures of dummy cartridges issued, namely:—

(a) Ordinary, with wooden bullet, as issued to battalions for all drill purposes with the rifle

(b) Special, consisting of the S.A.A. with the propellant removed and circular holes drilled in the brass case for identification purposes. These are made in Army shops and are issued on the scale of five per gun.

(a) Is suitable for drill purposes only and NOT for stripping the gun.

(b) Is suitable for drill purposes and for stripping and assembling the gun.

A.R.O.'s 46, 139 and 321 are cancelled.

670—Accidents with Grenades.

An accident causing heavy casualties has recently occurred. It was due to the careless carrying of No. 5 Grenades in sandbags.

Whenever possible, all Grenades will be carried in their boxes.

If they have to be carried in bags of any nature, the officer, N.C.O. or man in command of the carrying party will be responsible for seeing that the safety pins are properly secured before the party marches off.

671—Lamps, Signalling.—*In continuation of A.R.O. 627.*

A certain number of Lucas and Fallolite Daylight Signalling Lamps are now becoming available, and issue is authorised to Signalling Schools for instructional purposes on the following scale:—

	Lucas.	Fallolite.
Army Headquarters	4	2
Corps Headquarters	2	2
Divisional Headquarters	4	2

Demands will be submitted through the usual channels, and lamps will be supplied as soon as they are available.

(3/4 (Q.A. 3), 2-3-17.)

672—Bell Sets—Issue of to Light Trench Mortar Batteries.

Bell sets will be issued to Light Trench Mortar Batteries on a preliminary scale of two per Battery. Indents will be forwarded through the usual channels.

The following instructions will be observed:—

(a) To ring the far station press the button. This cuts out your own bell and puts the Battery to line.

When the button is not pressed the bell is connected between the two lines, or line and earth, in which position a ring can be received from the far station.

(b) Only low resistance cable must be used for connecting up these bells. Twin armoured cable is preferable, and it can be obtained from the Divisional Signal Officer. For very short lines, Cable D. 3 may be used. If an earth circuit is used, the earths must be very good. A buried biscuit tin makes a good earth.

(c) The bell sets must be kept dry.

(d) When renewing cells they must be joined up in series.

(Q.O.S./501/17/A, 22-1-17.)

673—Pigeon Baskets—Issue of.

Approval is given for the issue of a new pattern pigeon basket on the scale of 100 per Corps. These baskets are smaller, more portable, and less conspicuous than those at present in use, and are designed for the special purpose of carrying two birds in an assault.

They cannot be substituted for the trench baskets, because they are too small to keep birds in for more than a few hours. They will, therefore, be held on Corps charge and will be issued to troops when required.

Indents will be submitted through the usual channels, and issues will be made as supplies become available.

(Q.M.G. 16 (Q.A. 3), 6-3-17.)

674—Horseshoe Boxes and Grenade Boxes—Return of.

All empty serviceable or repairable horseshoe boxes will be returned to Railheads for transmission to the Base.

All empty grenade boxes will be returned to Ammunition Railheads for transmission to Ammunition Bases.

Para. 351 (*f*), Fourth Army Standing Orders, is cancelled.

(O.S.A. 1/5710/3, 1-3-17.)

675—Stone Forks.

Stone Forks, hitherto supplied by A.O.D., for road purposes, will, in future, be supplied under arrangements made by D.G.T.

Those due on outstanding indents from A.O.D. will be completed as far as possible.

(O.S.A. 2/138, 23-2-17.)

676—Clothing—Heavy Branch Machine Gun Corps.

Approval is given for the issue of dark brown combination suits for the Heavy Branch Machine Gun Corps, to replace the dungaree, canvas, or khaki drill over-all at present authorised.

Indents for replacements will be sent to Ordnance Officers concerned, and issues will be made when stocks are available.

On replacement, the suits of dungaree, canvas, or khaki drill, will be returned to the Base.

(Q.M.G. 4/16 (Q.A. 3), 23-2-17.)

677—Tents—Wood Bottoms for.

In future, wood bottoms will not be issued for tents of any description, except for hospitals, from the 1st April to the 30th September, inclusive.

(O.S.A. 2/25/9, 6-3-17.)

678—Empty Sacks.

Empty sacks which have contained any A.S.C. supplies are required at the Bases for re-filling, and will be returned to railhead as soon as possible.

679—Matches.—*Reference G.R.O. 1235.*

The scale of issue of Matches will be reduced to three boxes per man per fortnight, with effect from the week beginning 11th March, 1917.

H. C. HOLMAN, *Major-General,*
D.A. & Q.M.G., Fourth Army.

NOTICE.

Lost.

Between Pont Noyelles and Lahoussoye, between 5 and 6 p.m. on 26th February, 1917, a motor cycle tool kit.

Information to No. 1 Water Tank M.T. Company.

No. 61.

ROUTINE ORDERS

BY

GENERAL SIR H. S. RAWLINSON, Bart.,

K.C.B., K.C.V.O., Commanding Fourth Army.

16th April, 1917.

ADJUTANT GENERAL'S BRANCH.

846—SANITATION.

General Remarks.

1.—The approach of warmer weather makes it imperative that all ranks should appreciate the necessity for taking every possible precaution to safeguard the health of the troops during the coming summer.

It must be impressed upon all ranks that their comfort and immunity from preventable disease will depend upon the cleanliness of their surroundings, and more especially upon the destruction and non-accumulation of all matter which can attract, or afford a breeding place for, flies. Every man must do his share of this necessary work, and the responsibility for seeing that it is done must be extended down to the commanders of platoons and other small units.

2.—During the offensive of last year certain epidemic diseases gained a considerable hold, and there is good reason to believe that most formations which took part in the Battle of the Somme include men who are carriers of disease germs. The universal and conscientious observance of the rules of sanitation is, therefore, necessary, if an epidemic of a serious nature is to be warded off.

3.—The diseases in question, the most prevalent of which is Dysentery, all belong to the so called "Enteric" group. The germs which cause these diseases are spread through the fæces and urine of patients—early cases, slight cases, convalescents and "carriers." The diseases are literally caught by the swallowing of infected matter introduced into the mouth in water, or in food contaminated by flies, dust, mud or dirty hands. The sanitary measures detailed below all aim at the prevention of this swallowing of filth.

4.—It is a breakdown of ordinary sanitation which is most to be feared and guarded against. When excreta lie exposed and are trodden about, when flies swarm from latrines to cookhouses and to uncovered food, or when shell-hole water is the only water available, then infection is inevitable.

5.—If, on the other hand, the value and object of the sanitary measures and rules laid down in this order are correctly appreciated by all ranks, and if the sanitary organisation of units is sound and efficient, preventable disease will be reduced to a minimum.

Responsibility.

6.—The commander of every formation and unit is responsible for taking all measures necessary for the preservation of the health of those under him. He is responsible that each officer and soldier observes all sanitary orders, and that quarters and localities occupied by the troops under his command are kept and left in a clean and sanitary condition, no matter how short the period for which they may be occupied.

Commanding Officers will be held responsible that:—

(*a*) All officers and N.C.O.s are instructed in the principles of sanitation, and that they are acquainted with the orders bearing upon it.

(*b*) Sanitary personnel, as laid down by establishment for the units, are properly trained in sanitary duties, and are given every facility for, and assistance in, the execution of those duties.

Water.

7.—It is only by the maintenance of a sufficient and safe supply of water, under the supervision of medical officers and the specially trained personnel attached to them for this purpose, that men can be protected from the dangers of drinking water from shell holes and other foul sources.

8.—All water for cooking and drinking purposes must invariably be chlorinated before use, and must, whenever possible, be drawn from the service water-carts of the units.

9.—When the supply is stored or carried in petrol-tins, improvised vessels, or tanks, the storage, filling and cleansing of these receptacles, and the chlorination of the water, will be carried out under the supervision of the medical officer and the trained water-duty men of the unit.

10.—All water-carts are to be supplied with ample quantities of bleaching and clarifying powders. Every medical officer in charge of a unit is to have both chlorine and metallic test-cases in proper working order.

11.—Medical officers will invariably test all new sources of drinking-water, both for chlorine absorption, and for the presence of poisons. If the presence of poison is discovered or suspected, a sample of the water will be forwarded to the Mobile (Hygiene) Laboratory, attached Fourth Army Headquarters, by the most rapid means available. Local precautions only will be taken pending confirmation.

12.—All sources of supply will be distinctly marked with notice-boards showing whether the water is fit for drinking or not, as follows:—

> **DRINKING WATER.**
> REQUIRES * MEASURES BLEACHING POWDER PER WATER-CART.

* The number of measures required to be inserted here.

> **UNFIT FOR DRINKING.**

A stock of these notices will be kept by Sanitary Sections.

13.—In the case of wells found in areas reconquered from the enemy, each well required for use will be treated by the processes detailed below, in the order named:—

(a) Cleared of débris as far as possible.
(b) Disinfected by having about half a barrel of freshly burnt lime thrown into it. The water will then be stirred up thoroughly. When the well is so deep that stirring is impracticable, the lime must be added in solution, and the steining will be scrubbed down with the resulting milk of lime.
(c) Pumped out, allowed to re-fill, and treated with a second supply of lime.
(d) Allowed to stand for 24 hours.
(e) Pumped out again, after a thorough stirring, and allowed to refill. No more lime is to be added, and the well should be pumped out until there is no lime in the water.

14.—Where lime is unobtainable, chlorinated lime will be used in quantities sufficient to make a one per cent. solution. The calculation required to enable this disinfection to be carried out will be based on the following formula:—

$$D^2 \times .7854 \times d \times 6.25 \text{ gallons of water in the well, where } D = \text{diameter of well in feet.}$$
$$d = \text{depth of water in well in feet.}$$

15.—Steining which has been partly demolished should be rebuilt in brickwork and cement, with a backing of puddled clay and a facing of cement to a depth of 12 feet, when possible.

16.—All wells should be provided with a coping of masonry one foot high and a properly fitting cover. If a windlass and bucket are the only available means of raising water, the cover should be hinged.

17.—Every endeavour should be made to clear the ground round the well from refuse, etc. A well draws roughly an area having a radius of twice its depth.

18.—Tests, made with the Water Testing Case, to ascertain the amount of bleaching powder required to sterilise the water for drinking purposes, should be carried out at least daily until a fairly constant figure is obtained.

Food.

19.—Food must be protected from dust and dirt, and stored as far as possible in fly-proof cupboards or boxes. Gauze or butter muslin for the purpose will be obtained through Ordnance Officers. The indents will first be submitted to the Administrative Medical Officer concerned, who will certify that the quantities demanded are not in excess of actual requirements.

20.—All food-stores and cookhouses are to be kept scrupulously clean. Each cookhouse is to be provided with a proper grease-trap and a covered receptacle for refuse.

21.—No man who has suffered from Enteric or Dysentery is to be employed in the handling or cooking of food.

Cooks will be given every facility for keeping themselves and their premises clean, and will be provided with clean linen overalls.

22.—Men must be taught the necessity for cleanliness in eating, handling, and storing their food.

Latrines.

23.—Whilst on the move, and as a temporary measure, units will use shallow straddle-trench latrines of regulation type. Excreta are to be covered with earth at once.

24.—Permanent latrines, on the public system, will be made as soon as possible directly movement ceases. They will be either:—

(a) Deep trench latrines, eight feet deep by two feet wide, with fly-proof covers provided with self-closing lids;

or, if these are undesirable, owing to the danger of infecting water-supplies, to low-lying ground, or to lack of space,

(b) Buckets under fly-proof covers, with incineration of excreta.

The practice of putting a small latrine in the back garden of each billet is forbidden.

Urinals.

25.—Urinals of the deep covered-in type will be made near each latrine, and at other suitable spots, *e.g.*, near canteens, etc.

Night-urine pails will be provided for each billet.

Flies.

26.—The diseases from which armies suffer most severely are largely spread by flies, which carry infectious filth from latrines, etc., and deposit it upon food.

This danger will be guarded against by:—
   (a) Destroying the flies themselves with fly-traps, poisons, sprays, etc.
   (b) Destroying their breeding-places—fresh horse manure and food refuse.
   (c) Preventing their access to excreta by making latrines fly-proof.
   (d) Covering all food.

27.—Fly traps will be obtained through Ordnance Officers.

28.—Fly papers will be obtained through Supply Officers.

Horse Manure.

29—Ninety per cent. of all flies lay their eggs in fresh horse manure. During the succeeding 48 hours the eggs hatch into maggots, from which flies eventually emerge. To prevent this, every effort will be made to dispose of all fresh manure. This can be effected by one or both of the following methods:—

(a) Burning the Manure.

This is the better method and can be carried out without great difficulty even when there are large numbers of horses, provided that the fires are carefully tended, that the fresh manure is spread evenly in a thin layer over the burning heaps, and that large amounts of wet mud and manure scraped from horse-lines in rainy weather are carted away and not dumped on the fires.

(b) Close-packing the Manure.

The manure is carted away daily to a dump, where it is tightly stacked and firmly beaten down into regular heaps 10-ft. square and 5-ft. high.

The ground upon which the heap is to be stacked is thoroughly treated with wood-preserving oil, and the heap, while fresh, is sprayed each evening with a solution—Cresol one volume, paraffin or wood-preserving oil 20 volumes, water 79 volumes.

30.—Fresh manure belonging to civilians will, as far as possible, be removed and treated in a similar manner.

31.—Old heaps of manure, both of military and civilian origin, should be left alone. Fresh manure is not to be added to them.

Refuse.

32.—All waste food, empty tins, and refuse generally will be carefully collected and burned every day, except in the trenches, where refuse will be buried, special care being taken to ensure that it is covered up before flies lay their eggs upon it.

33.—Units will improvise incinerators in their billeting areas.

34.—Covered receptacles or bags will be placed wherever refuse is likely to accumulate.

Cleanliness of Ditches, etc.

35.—Each unit is responsible for the cleanliness of the ditches, streams, etc., near its billets and wagon lines. Tins and other rubbish are not to be thrown into them, and no dam is ever to be built to hold up the flow of water.

36.—Ditches already blocked by tins, etc., will be dug out at once. Grass and weeds must be cut away, and a systematic inspection carried out, so that drainage may be established and maintained.

37.—Mud is injurious to the health of men and animals, and must be removed promptly from billets.

Evacuation of Quarters, Billets, Camps or Bivouacs.

38.—When quarters are vacated, if tactical conditions permit, and civil labour is not requisitioned by Area Commanders, each unit will leave not more than 10 men, under a N.C.O., in addition to the men detailed to the Train vehicles, with the necessary tools, to fill in latrines and clear up the ground. The men left behind will march with the Baggage. Sites of latrines will be marked by a large letter "L" formed of stones, or by a notice-board.

H. C. HOLMAN, *Major-General*,
D.A. & Q.M.G., Fourth Army.

No. 62.

ROUTINE ORDERS

BY

GENERAL SIR H. S. RAWLINSON, Bart.,

K.C.B., K.C.V.O., Commanding Fourth Army.

20th April, 1917.

ADJUTANT GENERAL'S BRANCH.

847—Court-Martial.

On 3rd March, 1917, No. 70715 Private W. ROBINSON, The Sherwood Foresters, after being warned to take part in a forthcoming action, absented himself from his company, which was in the reserve position. He remained absent till 9th March, 1917, thereby avoiding the action. He was arrested at ETAPLES Station, after alighting from a train coming from PARIS. He was tried by Field General Court-Martial on 24th March, 1917, for "deserting his Majesty's Service" and was sentenced "to suffer death by being shot." The sentence was duly carried out at 6.45 a.m. on 10th April, 1917.

848—Commissions.

No candidates will be accepted for permanent commissions in the Royal Artillery until further notice, unless they have either been trained at a school of instruction in England, or have served in the ranks of a Royal Artillery unit for at least one year.

The case of those candidates who have been attached to batteries for instructional purposes is under consideration. They should, accordingly, remain with their batteries until the termination of the period of attachment. A report on their qualifications will then be forwarded in the usual way, and the candidates will be returned to their units.—(M.S. to C.-in-C. 510/13557, 12-4-17.)

A.R.O. 618 is cancelled.

849—Indian Army Promotion.

The Secretary of State for India in Council, with the concurrence of the Army Council, has, as a special measure, approved the introduction of the following time-scale for the **substantive** promotion of officers of the Indian Army and Indian Army Reserve during the present war:—

Promotion from Captain to Major after 15 years' service for promotion.
Promotion from Lieutenant to Captain after 4 years' service for promotion.
Promotion from Second Lieutenant to Lieutenant after 1 year's service for promotion.

The conditions of promotion to the substantive rank of Lieutenant-Colonel will remain unaltered.

Promotion under this measure will not be given from an earlier date than 1st September, 1915, and will not carry pay and allowances from an earlier date than 1st September, 1916. Between 1st September, 1915, and 1st September, 1916, such promotions, though not carrying pay, will be effective for purposes of wound, injury or family pensions or gratuities.

Promotion in each individual case will be subject to the officer being reported fit for promotion

On the conclusion of the war, officers will not be eligible for promotion to a higher rank than they then hold, until they have completed the ordinary period of service for promotion laid down in paragraph 318, Army Regulations, India, Vol. II.

The temporary rank of Captain or Major (without pay as such), after 6 and 16 years' service, respectively, previously granted as a war measure, will now cease to be operative, as officers will receive substantive promotion from the same or earlier dates.

The Special India Army Order of 19th June, 1916, regarding the promotion of officers of the Indian Army Reserve, will remain in force, subject to the necessary modification as regards paragraph 18 (a), the period of service qualifying for promotion therein referred to being reduced, subject to the conditions now notified, to one, four, and 15 years for the ranks of Lieutenant, Captain and Major, respectively.

The rules regarding acting promotion of officers on Field Service are not affected by the measure now announced.

Officers are not entitled to assume higher rank on completing the above-mentioned periods of service until their promotion has been notified either in Expeditionary Force Orders, the "Gazette of India," or "The London Gazette."

Antedates of rank and retrospective promotions due under the measure will now be gazetted as soon as possible, but some interval must necessarily elapse in those cases in which recommendations as to fitness for promotion have to be obtained.

Retrospective adjustments of pay becoming due in consequence of these promotions will be made as soon as practicable after the appearance of the Gazette notification of promotion.
(India Office Communiqué, dated 3-4-17.)

The names of all officers of the Indian Army and Indian Army Reserve of officers, who have completed:—

More than 1 years' service and less than 4 years' service,
More than 4 years' service and less than 15 years' service,
More than 15 years' service,

and who are thus eligible for retrospective substantive promotion to the next higher rank, in accordance with the above communiqué, will be submitted to the Military Secretary, General Headquarters, with a report as to whether they are recommended for such promotion or not.

In future, as an officer becomes eligible for substantive promotion to the next higher rank, on completion of 1, 4 or 15 years' service, as the case may be, a report will be submitted to the Military Secretary, General Headquarters, as to whether he is, or is not, recommended for such promotion.—(M.S. to C.-in-C. 11184, 10-4-17.)

850—Posting of Territorial Force Officers on joining the Forces Abroad.

It has been brought to notice that some T.F. officers, on joining a Force abroad, claim to be posted to a T.F. unit of their own regiment.

It should be made clear to all T.F. officers proceeding overseas as reinforcements that, where the exigencies of the service admit, they will be posted to their own T.F. units.

It cannot, however, be guaranteed that they will be so posted, and their services may have to be utilised elsewhere in the best interests of the Army.—(A.C.I. 587, 6-4-17.)

851—Advances to Officers.

(a) The arrangement by which officers now cash cheques through the Bank of France will cease on 1st May.

(b) From the same date, Field Cashiers may make advances to officers, above the rank of Captain, up to a total of Frs. 600 a month. Officers of the rank of Captain, and below, may continue to obtain advances up to Frs. 375 a month.

(c) The various Branches of Messrs. Cox & Co., Ltd. (France), at :—

PARIS	22, Rue Louis le Grand.
BOULOGNE	61, Rue Victor Hugo.
ROUEN	7, Rue Jeanne d'Arc.
HAVRE	122, Rue de Paris.
MARSEILLES	7, Rue Cannebiere.
AMIENS	Rue de l'Amiral Courbet (to be opened shortly).

will continue to cash cheques drawn on the authorised Agents, Messrs. Cox & Co., Messrs. Holt & Co., and Messrs. Sir C. R. McGrigor, Bart. & Co., as before.

852—Motor Headlights.

All motor headlights are to be extinguished in the vicinity of ammunition railheads.

QUARTERMASTER GENERAL'S BRANCH.

853—Boxed Ammunition.

To prevent waste and facilitate the removal of dumps in the event of an advance, field ammunition should be left boxed as long as possible. It should only be unboxed to meet immediate requirements.

854—Grenade Carriers.—*Continuation of A.R.O. 794.*

If an issue is desired of the waistcoat pattern grenade carrier, referred to in G.R.O. 1572, demands, to complete to 96 per Infantry battalion, will be submitted through the Ordnance officers concerned.—(Q.M.G. 10/33 (Q.B. 2), 22-3-17).

855—S.A. Cartridges for use with Rifle Grenades.

(i.) The rifle grenade cartridges now in use are :—
    (a) The ordinary 35-grain cartridges, mouth filled with *wax*.
    (b) Mark VII., unbulleted, mouth filled with *tallow*.

(ii.) It is found that no cartridge which has the mouth filled with wax can safely be employed with rifle grenades, and the use of such cartridges will cease.

(iii.) The Mark VII. cartridge gives a large proportion of blinds with Nos. 3, 20 and 24 grenades. The 35-grain cartridge will, therefore, be used with these three types of grenades, but the wax will be removed and replaced by tallow.

(iv.) Arrangements will be made by units and ammunition railhead Ordnance officers for the conversion of the 35-grain cartridge.

Tallow for the purpose will be demanded from ammunition railheads.—(10/4 (Q.B. 2), 10-4-17.)

856—Indents—Trench Mortar Batteries.

Indents for Ordnance stores for a trench mortar battery will, in future, only be recognised if submitted by the officer commanding the battery.—(O.S.A. 1/125, 11-4-17.)

857—Cartridge Containers for 3-in. Stokes Mortars.

Cartridge containers for 3-in. Stokes mortar ammunition of an outside diameter of $1\frac{5}{16}$-in. have been re-introduced for use with the new ring charges.

The $1\frac{7}{16}$-in. containers already manufactured may also be used.—(Q.M.G. 36/2 (Q.B.2), 14-4-17.)

858—3-in. Stokes Mortars.

An extractor, for removing the cartridge from the container, will be issued to trench mortar batteries and schools on a scale of one per 3-in. Stokes mortar.

Indents will be submitted to the Ordnance officers concerned.

The tools are being manufactured locally, and Ordnance officers of formations will indent on the Ordnance Officer, Fourth Army Troops, for their requirements.

183 I.M.B.

183rd Brigade Orders.
5-1-17 to 9-6-17.

Number 2.

No. 91.

Brigade Routine Orders by :-

BRIGADIER GENERAL A.H.SPOONER.D.S.O.   5.1.17.

COMMANDING 183rd. INFANTRY BRIGADE.

---

321. **HONOURS & AWARDS.**

The following extracts from Supplement to the London Gazette, dated 1st. January, 1917, are published for information.

To be Brevet Lieut-Colonel.

Major (Temp. Brig.-Gen.) A.H.Spooner, D.S.O.

Military Cross.

Capt. M.M.Parry-Jones, Roy.Fus. Bde.Major 183rd.Inf.Bde
2/Lieut. (Temp.Capt.) N.Thacker, 2/4th. Bn.Gloucester Regt. attd.T.M.B.
2/Lieut. (Temp.Capt.) G.S.Tomkinson, 2/7th.Bn. Worcester Regt.

Distinguished Conduct Medal.

No.2666, Sgt. G.E.Lait, 2/4th.Bn.Gloucester Regt.

322. **MACKINTOSH CAPES.**

Attention of all concerned is directed to D.R.O. No.721 dated 4th. January 1917.

323. **PERMANENT WORKING PARTIES.**

Special attention is directed to D.R.O.No.710 dated 3rd. January 1917.

324. **DISCIPLINE.**

During the past week 83 breaches of Traffic Regulations are reported by the A.P.M. as having occurred in the Corps area.

325. **TRAFFIC CONTROL.**

No passes for vehicles to proceed in a contrary direction to that laid down in Traffic Regulations may be issued without reference to Corps Headquarters.

326. **RANGEFINDERS.**

The attention of O.C. Machine Gun Coy. is directed to Fifth Army Routine Order No.343 dated 2.1.17.

327. **WIRE-CUTTERS AND HEDGING GLOVES.**

Attention has been drawn to the comparatively small number of wire-cutters and hedging gloves returned at the conclusion of the recent operations. These articles are difficult to obtain and every effort must be made to avoid loss and to salve those left on the battlefield.

(Sgd) P.V.Davies, Capt.
A/Staff Capt. 183rd. Infantry Bde.

No. 122.

BRIGADE ORDERS by :-
BRIGADIER GENERAL A.H.SPOONER D.S.O.
COMMANDING 183rd. INFANTRY BRIGADE.   26.5.17.

===

498. FIELD GENERAL COURT MARTIAL.

        A Field General Court Martial composed as under will
        assemble at DAINVILLE at 2.30 pm on 27th. May 1917, to try the
        accused person named in the margin, and any other accused
        persons that may be brought before it.

No.257189 Private J.   PRESIDENT. Lieut.Col. R.E.DOBSON, 2/4th.Glous.
BRINDIRHALO, 2/6th.
Bn.Gloucestershire   MEMBERS.   A Captain to be detailed by 2/4th.Glous.
Regiment.
                              "   "   "   "   "   "   " 2/7 Worc.

        The accused to be warned and all witnesses duly required
to attend.

        The 2/4th. Gloud. will arrange for a room and the necessary
stationery, and will also detail an Orderly to the Court.

        Proceedings will be forwarded to 183rd. Bde.H.Q.

499. PETROL TINS.

        VI Corps Routine Order No.2170 dated 19th May 1917, is
republished for information.

        "In order to economise petrol tins, each Division and each
        "Town Major will establish at once special 2 gallon petrol
        "tin Salvage Dumps, if they have not already done so.   The
        "map location of these dumps will be reported to this H.Q.
        "for insertion in Corps Routine Orders.
        "All Units in VI Corps will then be responsible for salving
        "all 2 gallon petrol tins, in the vicinity of their billets,
        "and returning them to the nearest dump. Divisions and
        "Town Majors will keep a special record of receipts and
        "issues of petrol tins at these dumps and will report
        "weekly to this H.Q. the total number received and how
        "disposed of".

        Reference above a special dump has been selected at
L.28.d.4.5. (near Enclenwater), and all salved petrol tins
will be deposited there.

Entered in Battery Orders

500. CHURCH SERVICES. Sunday 27th. May 1917.

        HOLY COMMUNION. at 8 am in the Y.M.C.A.Hut.

        Parade Service for Bde.H.Q. at 10 am in the Y.M.C.A.Hut.

B.H.Q.   (Sd) C.E.W.BOWEN   Captain.
26.5.17.   Staff Captain, 183rd. Infantry Bde.

                           NOTICE.

        The VI Corps CINEMA is now open in the Theatre, ARRAS.
        Prices as follows :-   Officers 1 franc.
                                Other Ranks 50 centimes & 25 centimes
        Two entertainments daily, afternoon 2.30 to 4.30 pm., evening
        6 to 8 pm. Doors open at 2 pm and 5.30 pm.

No. 134.

BRIGADE ORDERS by :-

BRIGADIER-GENERAL A.H. SPOONER, D.S.O.   29-5-1917.

COMMANDING 183rd. INFANTRY BRIGADE.

---

493. HONOURS & AWARDS:

Under authority granted by His Majesty The King, (M.S.H. 2260, dated 2-6-16) the G.O.C. IV Corps, has awarded the following decoration :-

MILITARY MEDAL - (Date of award 26-5-1917).

No. 14329, Sgt. R.W. COOK, 183rd M.G. Coy.

494. ESTIMATED CASUALTIES:

The attention of all concerned is directed to Divisional Routine Order No. 1165, dated 28th May, 1917.

The following extract from Bgd Order is republished for information of all ranks

495. BURIAL RECORD:

VI Corps Routine Order No. 2213 dated 26th May, 1917, is republished for information and guidance :-

The records of all burials in the Corps Area on and after 9th April, 1917, are being registered at Corps Headquarters.

It is particularly requested that any information regarding burials of any officers and other ranks, especially those undertaken by the unit or by friends, in single and isolated graves, should be communicated forthwith to this office. This information should always be given if there is any possible doubt of the grave being properly registered. Officers Commanding Units and Chaplains especially should send any information they can on this subject.

This information is at the disposal of all officers and men of units, who should apply through the usual channels. The details required may not always be immediately available, but any enquiries will be attended to as soon as possible. The names of any missing men should be submitted with a view to ascertaining if any have been killed in action. All Communications on registration should be earmarked "Burials" and should be sent to Corps Headquarters.

Communications regarding the actual burying will still be sent to the Corps Burial Officer.

This order will be republished in Battalion orders.

Enter in Battery Orders.

(sd) G.E.W. BOWYER,

B.H.Q.   Captain,
29-5-17.   Staff Captain, 183rd. Infantry Brigade.

S E C R E T.   Copy No. 17.

ADMINISTRATIVE ADDENDUM
to 183rd. Infantry Brigade Order No.123 of 31st. May 1917.

Map Reference 1/40,000 (Sheet 51c & 51b).   31st. May 1917.

1. **SUPPLIES.**
    (a) <u>Railroad</u>. June 2nd. and onwards - ARRAS (Goods Station). Supplies will be drawn from Railhead by Horse Transport on completion of move.

    (b) On June 2nd. 183rd. Inf.Bde. Group Refilling Point will move to FAUBOURG de BAUDIMONT, ARRAS (G.20.c.5.4.) Time of Refilling will be notified later.

    (c) Coal Dump at G.20.b.3.8.

2. <u>TRANSPORT</u> Lines of all Units of 183rd. Inf.Bde. are at ACHICOURT. Route to Support Bde.H.Q. (TILLOY) is through BEAURAINS.
    N.B. No Transport Lines can be North of a line running East and West through L.22.central. L.23.central. L.24. central. G.19.central. G.20.central on account of the danger area of the Rifle Range.
    N.B. Units will take over Transport Lines and Q.M. Stores of the corresponding Units of the 63rd.Inf.Bde.

3. <u>AMMUNITION DUMPS.</u>
    (a) The Main Divisional Bomb Store, under Lieut.LESSITER at X Roads H.8.d.7.8. (with Reserve Divisional Bomb Store at Chester Cave G.28.b.8.1.).

    (b) <u>Brigade Dumps.</u>

1. TANK Dump	....	N.18.a.4.8.
2.	....	O. 7.b.8.2.
3. REAR Dump	....	N.16.c.8.5.
4.	....	N.12.b.5.0.
5. LA BERGERE Cellars	....	N.12.d.2.9.
6. Near Left Bn.H.Q.	....	N.12.d.2.8.
7. Right Support H.Q.	....	N.17.d.1.2.
8. Centre Front H.Q.	....	N.11.d.central.

    The contents of these dumps is unknown but Units will draw direct therefrom by Indent signed by an Officer.

4. <u>R.E.DUMPS</u>. Main Dump RITZ (G.29.a.0.0.)
    Advanced Dump WANCOURT (N.16.a.4.9.)

    All Indents will be countersigned by the Staff Captain or a R.E.Officer.

5. <u>WATER SUPPLY</u>.
    Transport waters from troughs at ACHICOURT.

Water Carts.	Taps.	Horse Troughs.
G.23.d.5.8.	H.3.a.1.9.	G.29.a.
H.31.a.9.3.	H.31.a.9.3.	G.29.central.
G.27.a.8.8.	G.28.a.8.6.	H.32.d.
G.28.a. 35.65.	G.28.b.10.70.65	G.27.a.9.9.
G.23.d.05.25.	G.22.c.50.95.	G.20.d.3.5.
H.31.c.2.2.	G.28.a.85.65.	H.31.c.0.0.
	G.28.a.4.8.	G.36.d.0.0.
	G.28.b.1.6.	
	G.28.a.90.38.	
	G.28.d.7.3.	
	G.28.d.05.60.	
	G.14.c.10.05.	
	G.28.d.9.7.	

                1.   P.T.O.

6. ROADS.

    1. The TILLOY - WANCOURT Road is good for all Traffic and will be used in preference to the CAMBRAI Road.

    2. Horse Traffic does not proceed through WANCOURT, but Pack animals are taken as far as Battalion H.Q.

    3. There is a fair weather Track through G.35.a.8.b. - M.6.c. to X roads at M.8.d.7.8.: also a footway from G.29.c.2.1. to M.6.b. central.

7. STRAGGLER POSTS.

    The line of Divisional Straggler Posts will be along the road from M.3.d.6.8. to FEUCHY.

8. MEDICAL ARRANGEMENTS.

    A.D.S. TILLOY.

    Main Dressing Station. HOPITAL ST. JEAN - Rue ST.AUBERT - ARRAS.

    Bearer Posts. at M.11.a.7.7. & at M.17.d.3.4.

    Regimental Aid Posts. at M.12.c.7.4. & at M.18.d.5.5.

9. ORDNANCE.

    D.A.D.O.S. will be at 40 Rue D'AMIENS, ARRAS from June 2nd. inclusive.

    32 Ordnance Mobile Workshop is in the RUE DE LA PAIX - ARRAS.

10. VETERINARY.

    61st. Mobile Vet.Section will remain for the present with the 61st. R.A. The Mobile Vet.Section of the 50th. Div. situated at ACHICOURT & AGNY will receive animals of Units requiring treatment or evacuation.

11. BATHS.

    (a) Officers. - RUE GAUGIERES, ARRAS.
        Other Ranks. - SCHRAMM BARRACKS, ARRAS.

    (b) There are also Baths at TILLOY.

12. CANTEENS.

    Divisional Canteen opens on June 2nd. at 63 RUE ST.AUBERT. E.F.C. at 44 MAISON BLEUE, RUE ST.AUBERT.

13. KITS.

    The Divisional Surplus Kit Store will remain at DOULLENS.

14. SALVAGE.

    Salvage Section works under the Corps Salvage Officer.
    Corps Dump - G.29.c.1.3.

15. ARTILLERY.

    The following formations are attached to the Division :-

        3rd. Division Artillery.
       12th.   "   "
      155th. Field Artillery Brigade.

16. **PACK SADDLES**.

Units will take over all Pack Saddles extra to Mobilization Establishment from the Units of the 37th. Div. they relieve.

Receipts will be given for these and the numbers so taken over will be reported to Brigade H.Q.

17. **ACKNOWLEDGE**.

G.E.W.Bowyer
Captain.
Staff Captain, 183rd. Infantry Bde.

B.H.Q.
31.5.17.

Issued at 2.30 pm.

Copy Nos. 1 to 6 Bdo. Staff.
" Nos. 7 & 8 4/Glouc.
" " 9 & 10 6/Glouc.
" " 11 & 12 7/Worc.
" " 13 & 14 8/Worc.
" " 15 & 16 183 M.G.Coy.
" " 17 183 T.M.B.

Copy No. 18 to No.3 Coy. Div. Train.
" " 19 " 478 Fld. Coy. R.E.
" " 20 " 3rd. Fld. Amb.
" " 21 " Bde. Transport Offr.
" " 22 " Bde. Q.M.S.
" " 23 " Bde. Group Supply Offr.

No. 135.

BRIGADE ORDERS by:-

BRIGADIER-GENERAL A.H. SPOONER, D.S.O. 2-6-17.

COMMANDING 183rd. INFANTRY BRIGADE.

---

496. CHURCH SERVICES:

Sunday 3rd. June 1917, Wesleyans and Nonconformists in the wood near TILLOY Church at 10 a.m.

497. RETURN OF CANADIANS:

The Canadian Authorities are desirous of obtaining certain information from every Canadian Officer and man in the Field.

Numbers of Canadians by Units will be reported to Brigade H.Q., on, or before, Monday June 4th.

498. COURT-MARTIAL:

No. 8733 Pte (L/Cpl) W. BROOM, Suffolk Regiment, and No. 7471 Pte. A. ELSEGOOD, Norfolk Regiment, were seen coming out of a house in ARRAS. On being searched they were found to be in possession of a number of articles belonging to the owner of the house.

They were tried by Field General Court-Martial on a charge of theft, under Section 6 (I.) (f) of the Army Act, both were found guilty and sentenced to six months I.H.L., which sentence has been put into execution.

This order will be republished in the orders of all units.

499. R.E. DUMPS ETC. :

Reference Administrative Addendum to 183rd. Infantry Brigade Order No. 123, dated 31st May 1917.
Para. 4 R.E.Dumps etc.
This should read:-
"All Indents must be signed by a R.E. Officer" (NOT by the Staff Captain).

B.H.Q.
2-6-17.

(signed) G.E.W. Graham,
Staff Captain, 183rd. Infantry Brigade.

No. 136.

BRIGADE ORDERS BY:-

BRIGADIER-GENERAL A.H. SPOONER, D.S.O.   6-6-17.

COMMANDING 123rd INFANTRY BRIGADE.

---

450. **STRENGTH RETURNS.**
Attention is directed to G.R.O., No. 2348 dated May 29th 1917.

451. **No. 27 PHOSPHORUS GRENADE; No. 31 SIGNAL RIFLE GRENADE (DAY); No. 32 SIGNAL RIFLE GRENADE (NIGHT).**
The above Grenades will shortly be available for issue.
The special attention of the troops will be drawn to the necessity for removing the cap cover after withdrawing the safety pin and before firing.
Unless this is done the sealing of the ventilation by the cap cover may result in premature explosion.
This warning will be communicated to all concerned before any issues of these types of Grenades are made.
The new edition of the cards of instruction contained in each box will include a note to this effect.—(Q.M.G. 10/25 (Q.B. 2), 24-4-17.).

452. **MILLS - OCCUPATION OF.**
In future no troops will be billeted in mills of any description, or in outhouses forming part of the mill buildings.   (VI Corps:- O. 26/3).

(Sd) G.E.W. BOWYER.
B.H.Q.   Capt.
6-6-17.   Staff Captain, 123rd Infantry Brigade.

SECRET.   Copy No. 14

183rd INFANTRY BRIGADE ORDER NO. 124.   9.6.1917.

Ref: Sheet 51b and c.

1. On the night 10th/11th June the 61st Division (less Artillery) will be relieved in the CAMBRAI Sector by the 56th Division.

2. The 183rd Brigade Group will move to SIMENCOURT in accordance with Table "A".

3. Route:- FBG. ST. SAUVEUR - ARRAS STATION - SCHRAMM Barracks - FBG. AMIENS - X Rds in R.8.c. - BERNEVILLE.

4. The following distances will be maintained on the march.

   In & East of ARRAS. - 300 yards between platoons and sections of Machine Gun Coy.

   West of ARRAS.   300 yards between Battalions, 100 yards between Companies.

5. The Brigade Transport will be brigaded, and march under orders of Brigade Transport Officer, to whom separate orders will be issued. A distance of 200 yards between the Transport of Units will be maintained.

6. Field Kitchens, Tool-carts, and Water Carts, at present with Battalions will return to the Transport Lines by 5 p.m. on the 10th instant.
   Fighting Limbers of M.G.Coy, Lewis Gun Limbers, and Baggage Wagons will march in rear of each Unit.

7. Separate orders will be issued as regards Billets and the handing over of Billet Stores. Receipts for stores handed over will be rendered to the Staff Captain by 6 p.m. 11th.

8. O.C. No. 3 Field Ambulance will detail 2 Horse Ambulances to follow in rear of R.E.Coy.

9. Each Battalion will detail a Rear Guard to march in rear of the Unit.

10. Brigade H.Q. close at TILLOY at 9 p.m. 10th, and open at SIMENCOURT at the same hour. Reports of completion of move will be rendered to SIMENCOURT.

11. ACKNOWLEDGE.   M. M. Parry-Jones.

                                              Capt.,
Issued at 1-30 pm.   Bde. Major, 183 Inf. Bde.

Copy No.1 - War Diary,
   "   2 to 8 - Bde.Staff.
   "   9 - 4 Glosters.
   "   10 - 6 Glosters.
   "   11 - 7 Worcesters.
   "   12 - 8 Worcesters.
   "   13 - 183 M.G.Coy.
   "   14 - 183 T.M.B.
   "   15 - 478 Field Coy, RE.
   "   16 - 3 Coy, Div.Train.
   "   17 - 3rd Fld. Amb.
   "   18 - 61 Div."G".
   "   19 - A.D.M.S.
   "   20 - C.R.E.
   "   21 - 182 Inf.Bde.
   "   22 - 184 Inf.Bde.
   "   23 -

MARCH TABLE "A" - ISSUED WITH 183rd INF. BDE. ORDER NO. 124 DATED 8.6.17.

Serial No.	Units in order of March.	TO	Starting Point.	Time.	Remarks.
1.	No. 3 Coy. Div. Train.	SAINCOURT.	Rd. Junction in G.25.b.	4 pm.	
2.	3 Fld. Amb.	ditto.	ditto	4-15 pm.	Transport to march in two parts at 100 yards distance, 250 yards in rear of personnel.
3.	7th Worcesters.	ditto	Rd.Junction G.26.b.2.8.	7.11 pm.	
4.	8th Worcesters.	ditto	Rd.Junction H.32.c.8.3.	7.31 pm.	
5.	6th Glosters.	ditto	X Rds.H.31.c.6½.½.	8.30 pm.	
6.	4th Glosters.	ditto	ditto	9.20 pm.	
7.	183 T.M.B.	ditto	Bde.H.Q. TILLOY.	10.10 pm.	
8.	183 M.G.Co.	ditto	As in 3.	10.25 pm.	
9.	478 Fld.Coy.RE.	ditto.	Factory L.35.b.	12 mdnt.	On relief at W.S.d.C.8. Will march in small parties to Transport lines in ACHICOURT and rest there until time for proceeding to Starting Point. Transport to march with Unit 250 yds in rear of personnel.

S E C R E T.   COPY NO... 15

ADMINISTRATIVE ADDENDUM
to 183rd. Infantry Brigade Order No.124 dated 8th. June 1917.

Reference Map 1/40,000, Sheets 51c & 51b.   8th. June 1917.

1. **SUPPLIES.**

DATE.	RAILHEAD.	REFILLING POINT.	REMARKS.
June 11th. & onwards.	AGNES LES DUISANS.	On SIMENCOURT - BERNEVILLE Road near BERNEVILLE.	Time:- 9 am. Guides from each Unit to attend on June 11th.

   NOTE. Coal dump on WARLUS - DAINVILLE Road near WARLUS.

2. **STORES.** Strombos Horns, Tents, Trench Shelters etc. will be handed over 'in Situ', & receipts sent to Bde.H.Q.
   NOTE. The Brigade Transport Officer will hand over all the tents, shelters etc. now occupied by the Brigaded Transport & will send a consolidated receipt to Bde.H.Q.
   Q.M's of Units billetted in ACHICOURT will obtain "clean billet" certificates.

3. **BILLETING.** The whole Brigade Group moves to SIMENCOURT.
   Billeting parties of all Units will find billeting papers awaiting them at Town Major's Office at SIMENCOURT at 10 am. on June 10th.

4. **TRANSPORT.** 3 Lorries will report to billet of Brigade Transport Officer at 7 am. on June 10th. & will be loaded under orders to be issued by him to Q.M's & T.O's of Units.
   Baggage wagons will be returned to Units on the afternoon of June 9th.

5. **AMMUNITION.** Units will move with S.A.A. & Bombs complete to Establishment. All deficiencies will be made up from Div.Bomb Store at N.8.d.6.8. BEFORE leaving present area.

6. **ORDNANCE.** Ordnance Stores will be at WARLUS.

7. **VETERINARY.** 61st. Mob.Vet.Section will be at WARLUS from 9th.June.

8. **MEDICAL ARRANGEMENTS.** Men who canNOT march and who must be carried will be at Cross Roads near 2/1st.Field Amb.(H.31.c.6.0) at 3 pm. Where they will await Motor Ambulances.

9. **ACKNOWLEDGE.**

                                                        G.E.W.Bowyer
                                                            Captain.
B.H.Q.   Staff Captain, 183rd. Infantry Brigade.
8.6.17.

Issued at 2.30 pm.

Copies No.	Unit		Copy No.	Unit
1 - 4	Bde.Staff.		17	2/3rd.Fld.Amb.
5 & 6	4/Glouc.		18	O.C.3 Coy.Div.Train.
7 & 8	6/Glouc.		19	183 Bde.Supply Offr.
9 & 10	7/Worc.		20	Bde.Transport Offr.
11 & 12	8/Worc.		21	Bde.Q.M.S.
13 & 14	183 M.G.Coy.		22	Town Major SIMENCOURT
Copy No. 15	183 T.M.B.		23	ACHICOURT.
16	478 Fld.Coy.R.E.			

No. 137.

BRIGADE ORDERS by:-
BRIGADIER-GENERAL A.H. SPOONER, D.S.O.   9-6-17.
COMMANDING 183rd INFANTRY BRIGADE.

---

453.   CHURCH SERVICES, SUNDAY JUNE 10th. 1917.

Nonconformist:
11-30 a.m. in the wood East of 2/1st Field Ambulance.

ROMAN CATHOLIC :- at 7.30 am in Ruined Church, TILLOY

454.   CARTRIDGES S.A.
It is notified for information that serious accidents have recently occurred with No. 23 (Mills) Rifle-Grenades owing to the use of unbulleted Mark VII S.A. cartridges, the mouths of which had not been filled with tallow.
Unless the mouth of the cartridge is filled with tallow the cordite is apt to be blown up the barrel without being ignited by the percussion cap. The result is that the grenade is only pushed a few inches out of the cup, but sufficiently far to release the lever, and the grenade explodes at or near the muzzle.
Instructions should be issued to all concerned that unbulleted cartridges are not to be used with rifle-grenades unless the mouth is filled with tallow.
(Authority Third Army 0/359 dated 4/6/17, VI Corps G/18/44).

455.   TOWN ORDERS - AREAS.
C.R.O. E259 dated 6th June, 1917, is republished for the information of all concerned :-
"Para. 10 of Town Orders, ARRAS, is republished for the information of all concerned -
"Lights.
"Lights in buildings must be invisible from the outside both back and front".
This order is to be republished in Battalion orders.

456.   AREA STORES - REMOVAL OF:
Corps R.O. E261 dated 6th June, 1917 is republished for information :-
"Corps R.O. No. E240 dated 1-6-17, para. (3) is amended to read as follows :-
"Units are forbidden to take away latrine or any other sanitary structures from areas where they have been erected by the Town Major or by any sanitary parties".
The above order is to be republished in Battalion orders.

B.H.Q.   (sd) G.E.W. BOWYER,   Capt.
9-6-17.   Staff Captain, 183rd Infantry Brigade.

183 T.M.B.

61st Divisional Orders.
February 1917.

R.

Number 4.

DIVISIONAL ROUTINE ORDERS
by
Major-General Colon Mackenzie, C.B.,
Commanding 61st Division.

---oOo---

Headquarters, 25th February, 1917.

857... DRINKING WATER

It has come to notice that it is a common practice amongst the troops to drink water obtained from shell-holes.

The result of analysis shows that this water is not fit to drink and liable to cause disease.

All ranks are warned that the drinking of such water, whether boiled or not, is strictly forbidden and disciplinary action will be taken against all offenders.

Sufficient clean and properly sterilised water for drinking purposes will be conveyed to the troops in petrol cans.

858... RAILWAYS:

Considerable damage is being done to light railway tracks by troops making use of them as thoroughfares, also by Artillery and Transport vehicles crossing the lines indiscriminately, instead of at the proper crossing places.

On no account are troops permitted to walk on the tracks except those actually employed working on the Railway.

Vehicles are not to be allowed to cross except at the proper crossing places.

Unit Commanders will take severe disciplinary action should any breach of these orders occur in future.

859... DENTURES:

Cases of loss or fracture of dentures supplied by Government to N.C.O's and men will be investigated by Officers Commanding Units.

All ranks concerned will be warned that they are liable to be tried by Court Martial if the result of such investigation shows wilful damage or negligence.

860... RATIONS:

Until further notice only half quantities of the usual proportion of Frozen Meat can be sent from the Base, - Preserved meat will be issued in lieu.

861... INOCULATION:

Units when in rest should take the opportunity of having all ranks re-inoculated when necessary.

862... TRAFFIC:

The MOREUIL-PLESSIER road is closed for all lorry traffic until further orders.

863... TOWN MAJORS: APPOINTMENT OF.

The following have been appointed Town Majors :-
2/Lieut. S. C. SQUIRES, 2/8 R. Warwicks, MARCELCAVE:
Capt. S. E. BROCK . . . 2/6 do. HARBONNIERES:
Capt. W. J. F. GRAIG, 2nd Field Amb. VAUVILLERS.
2/Lieut. E. W. HILL, 2/7 Worcesters, FRAMERVILLE.

These officers will assume duty on 26th February, 1917.
Town Majors for GUILLAUCOURT and WIENCOURT will be appointed later.

H. C. Brighton,
Lieut-Colonel,
A.A.&Q.M.G., 61st Division.

NOTICE:

FOUND :- Brown mule, black points, gelding, about 14-2: strayed to Transport Lines 2/8 Worcesters, FRAMERVILLE.

DIVISIONAL ROUTINE ORDERS,
by
Major-General Colin Mackenzie, C.B.,
Commanding 61st Division
----------oOo----------

Headquarters, 28th February, 1917.

872. STROMBOS HORNS.

Strombos horns will be located as follows:-

Right Bde: Bde. H.Q. 3 Bn. H.Qrs. and 9 Coy. H.Qrs. 13.
Left Bde: Bde. H.Q. 3 Bn. H.Qrs. and 11 Coy. H.Qrs. 15.

One each at - D.H.Q.
 Bn. H.Q. at - VAUVILLERS.
   RAINECOURT.
   FRAMERVILLE.
   HERLEVILLE.
   GUILLAUCOURT.
R.A. PLACE BLANCHE.
306th Bde. H.Q.
307th Bde. H.Q.
306th Wagon Lines.
307th Wagon Lines.
D.A.C. CAMP 84. W.23.a.
Train. W.20.b.
          13.
     TOTAL. 41.

There will also be one at Divisional Gas School for instructional purposes. Copies of Sentry's Orders will be supplied, and will be kept with each horn.

873. UNSERVICEABLE CLOTHING, BOOTS, ETC.

1. All unserviceable articles of S.D. clothing (including boots, which must be tied together in pairs) must be returned to the Divisional Ordnance Clothing Stores.
They will be accepted on any day between the hours of 2-0.p.m. and 4-0.p.m.
They will be checked in the presence of the unit returning them, and a receipt will be given by the A.O.D. representative.
2. All underclothing will be sent to the Divisional baths.

874. HUTS.

IV Corps Routine Order No. 1062 dated 27th February 1917, is republished for information.
"All huts taken over by Divisions from the French must be inspected by the R.E. to ensure that in fixing stoves, all possible precautions have been taken against fire".

875. DECAUVILLE SYSTEM. (Demands for use of).

1. Demands for use of Decauville System will be made by wire to:
 Lieut. BIRD,
  c/o Liaison Officer,
   Voie 60 c.m.,
    BEAUCOURT.
2. All wires will be repeated to IV Corps.
3. Demands should be made in the following form :
Transportation required for   tons of (Material) from   to   at (time).
4. Lieut. BIRD will inform the unit or formation the hour at which the material will be loaded.
5. The Decauville Lines will be open to traffic from March 1st inclusive.

876. TRAFFIC.
The FOUILLOY - AUBIGNY road is closed until further orders.

         Lieut-Colonel.
      A.A. & Q.M.G. 61st Division.

183 T.M.B.

61st Divisional Orders.
April 1917.

R

Number 5.

DIVISIONAL ROUTINE ORDERS
by
Major-General Colin MACKENZIE, C.B.,
Commanding 61st Division.
- - - - - - oOo - - - - - - -

Headquarters, 13th April, 1917.

1055...DIVINE SERVICES:
　　　　The following Services, C. of E., will be held on Sunday 15th April, 1917, at Divisional Headquarters, a-
　　　　9-15 a.m., Prayers in D.H.Q. Office;
　　　　10-0 a.m. Church Parade;
　　　　10-40 a.m. Holy Communion.
The two last named Services will be held in "MANCHESTER HALL" near Church, VOYENNES.

1056...HONOURS AND AWARDS:
　　　　The following award for gallantry has been made :-
　　　　MILITARY MEDAL. (Date of Award 12-4-1917).
No. 241643, Sergeant H. W. COLEMAN, 2/5th Bn. Gloucestershire Regiment. (T. F.).

1057...ORDNANCE MOBILE WORKSHOP (LIGHT).
　　　　No. 1: Ordnance Mobile Workshop, (Light), has now moved to the site recently occupied by D.A.D.O.S. at CROIX MALIGNAUX.
　　　　All guns, vehicles, etc., requiring attention should be sent there.

1058...UNSERVICEABLE ORDNANCE STORES:
　　　　A dump for the reception of these Stores has been established at J.20.a.7.7., and will be open daily from 10 to 12 a.m., and 2 to 4 p.m.
　　　　All unserviceable Ordnance Stores (including Service dress clothing clothing and boots, but excluding dirty underclothing - which will continue to be dealt with as laid down in D.R.O. 1031 dated 6-4-1917) will either be sent direct to this dump or handed in to Ordnance lorries at Ordnance refilling points.
　　　　Unserviceable stores must not be accumulated, but disposed of daily.

1059...FORAGE.
　　　　During the present inclement weather and until further notice the full ration of oats will be issued.
(Authority IV Corps wire No. Q.756 of 12.4.1917).

　　　　　　　　　　　　　　　　　　Lieut-Colonel,
　　　　　　　　　　　　　　　A.A.&.Q.M.G., 61st Division.

DIVISIONAL ROUTINE ORDERS
by
Major-General Colin Mackenzie, C.B.,
Commanding 61st Division.
- - - - - oOo - - - - -

Headquarters, 20th April, 1917.

1068... FIELD CASHIER:
The Field Cashier will attend at Divisional Headquarters, AUROIR, on Monday the 23rd instant - 2-30 to 4-30 p.m.

[margin: X for orders. One officer to attend. Put in orders Sunday night.]

1069... BOX RESPIRATORS, P.H.HELMETS & GOGGLES, INDENTS FOR:
All demands for Gas appliances will, in future, be made on A.F. G.994 in duplicate to Divisional Gas Officer, and if for replacement of unserviceable the unserviceable will be handed in to him at the same time.

After satisfying himself that the demand is in order, the Divisional Gas Officer will countersign the indent and pass one copy to the D.A.D.O.S., who will issue direct to the unit from his reserve stock.

[margin: Note:]

1070... DRIPPING:
Reference D.R.O. 991 of 23rd March, 1917.
The attention of all units is again drawn to Fourth Army Routine Order 715 of the 20th March, 1917.
While it is recognised that the fat on frozen meat has of late been scarce and such products have been much used by Units for the purpose of stock-pots and of making "Tommy's Cookers", the urgency of the supply of glycerine at Home for the manufacture of explosives must not be overlooked.

There is no difficulty in the case of units other than those holding the line in complying with the terms of this Army Order, and, with the approach of warmer weather the use of stock-pots by Units will not be necessary to the same extent as in the winter.

These tins will be forwarded by units on returning empty Supply wagons to Brigade Supply Officers, who will arrange for their forwarding to Railhead on Supply Column lorries.

O.C. Train will report to D.H.Q. on the last day of each month, the number of tins returned by each unit.

[margin: Inform the cookers about this.]

1071.... BATHS:
Divisional Baths will open at GERMAINE on the 24th April. Applications for use of Baths should be addressed to Divisional Baths Officer by 6 p.m. the evening previous to the day they are required.

Units in possession of dirty clothing will send it at once to the reception store at The Chateau, AUROIR.

[signatures]
Lieut-Colonel,
A.A.&Q.M.G., 61st Division.

NOTICE:

All French Interpreters will report for pay at the French Mission, Divisional Headquarters, on Monday, 23rd April, 1917, at 10-0 a.m.

DIVISIONAL ROUTINE ORDERS,
by
Major-General Colin Mackenzie, C.B.,
Commanding 61st Division.
----------oOo----------

Headquarters, 23rd April, 1917.

1077. **CARE OF FEET.**
Units in the line will draw at once from the foot baths at No. 27 billet, GERMAINE, a sufficient supply of camphor powder to sprinkle daily in the men's socks.

Troops proceeding to the trenches should make the necessary arrangements with the O.C. Baths to have the men's feet treated, and a supply of camphor powder issued.

It is notified for information that precautions against trench foot (not whale oil) are still in vogue.

[signature]

Lieut-Colonel.
A.A. & Q.M.G.,
61st Division.

NOTICES.

LOST: Chestnut mule, gelding, clipped "V" mark on neck near side. No headgear. 15 hands. No. 1245.

Chestnut female mule, clipped "V" mark on neck near side. White fetlocks both hind. Light Muzzle. 15.2.

Chestnut mule, gelding. White star, square mark, U.D. branded on off hind. Broad arrow near hind. 15.2.

Black horse, gelding, unnumbered. 14½.
Information to Headquarters, 61st Divisional Artillery.

DIVISIONAL ROUTINE ORDERS
by
Major-General Colin Mackenzie, C.B.,
Commanding 61st Division.
---------oOo---------

Headquarters, 24th April, 1917.

1078... RECORD OF OCCUPATION IN CIVIL LIFE.
The attention of Officers Commanding units is directed to Army Order 93 of March, 1917, (especially para. 6) and appendix issued therewith.

1079... LEAVE - SANITATION.
Fourth Army Routine Order No. 540 of 30th January, 1917, is republished for information :-
"Complaints have been received that soldiers are still reaching England in a verminous condition. It is necessary, therefore, that men, before proceeding on leave, should :-
(a) Bathe.
(b) Receive a complete set of clean clothing.
(c) Have all articles of their Service Dress disinfected.
Corps and Divisions will arrange for this to be done and every man granted leave will be given a certificate that he was free from vermin when he proceeded on leave."
Certificates will be given under Regimental arrangements.

1080... DOGS:
Attention is called to G.R.O's 1868 and 1964.

1081... TRAFFIC RESTRICTIONS - GUIDES FOR LORRIES:
When guides are sent to accompany lorries, it is necessary that such guides should be in possession of lorry traffic maps and able to instruct any lorry, when its services are no longer required, the route by which it should return.

1082... SALVAGE OF DOCUMENTS, RELICS, etc., IN AREAS EVACUATED BY THE ENEMY:
Any documents, relics, archives or valuables of any sort that may be found relating to houses or Churches should at once be handed over to the A.P.M. or French Mission.
Such articles should be labelled, showing clearly the village and, if possible, the site on which they were found.
Attention is also drawn to G.R.O. 1244.

1083... AGRICULTURAL IMPLEMENTS - COLLECTION OF:
Units should render every possible assistance to the French Mission in the collection of agricultural implements.

1084... WIRE - NOT TO BE THROWN INTO RIVERS & CANALS EXCEPT FOR TACTICAL PURPOSES:
Wire will not be thrown into rivers or canals, except for Tactical purposes.
Troops must be warned against this practice.

H. C. Singleton,
Lieut-Colonel,
A.A.&.Q.M.G., 61st Division.

NOTICE:

LOST: Plain wrist-watch between AUROIR and ETREILLERS on morning of 21st inst.
Information to Camp-Commandant.

DIVISIONAL ROUTINE ORDERS,
by
Major-General Colin Mackenzie. C.B.,
Commanding 61st Division.
--------oOo--------

Headquarters, 25th April, 1917.

1085. **FIELD GENERAL COURT MARTIAL.**
A Field General Court Martial, composed as under, will assemble at ETREILLERS, at 10-0.a.m. on Saturday, 28th April, for the trial of No. M.2/153002, Private G.A. PACK, A.S.C., (M.T.), attached 2/2nd (S.M.) Field Ambulance, and such other accused as may be brought before it.

PRESIDENT.

Major F.W. FOSTER, 2/5th Bn. Royal Warwickshire Regt.

MEMBERS.

A Captain, 183rd Inf. Bde.
A Subaltern, 184th Inf. Bde.

Accused will be warned, and all witnesses duly required to attend.
Proceedings will be forwarded to this office.

1086. **ACTING RANK. (Applications for).**
Divisional Routine Order No. 1009 is cancelled.
With reference to General Routine Order 2192 of 10th March, applications for the retention of acting rank should not be submitted until the relinquishment of the acting rank of Officers entitled to retain such acting rank has appeared in the London Gazette, on the re-adjustment of promotion.
The date of the London Gazette in which the relinquishment was announced should be quoted in the application for retention of acting rank.

1087. **BOUNDS. (Area occupied by the French).**
(For Battery Orders) No N.C.O. or man is to proceed into the area occupied by the French, unless he is properly dressed and in possession of a pass signed by his Commanding Officer.

1088. **BOUNDS. (Fields of growing crops or clover).**
(For Battery Orders) Fields of growing crops or clover are strictly out of bounds, and great care should be taken that animals are not permitted to graze in them.
Notice Boards prohibiting the use of such fields are to be erected where necessary. These can be obtained on application to the Divisional Sanitary Section.

1089. **CURRENCY. (Rate of Exchange).**
(For Battery Orders) Reference General Routine Orders 1698 and 2214, owing to notification of an approaching fall in the rate of exchange, Institutes are authorized to adjust the rate of Frs.27 C.25 per sovereign, from 25th April to 30th April, inclusive.

H.C. Singleton.

Lieut-Colonel.
A.A. & Q.M.G.,
61st Division.

183 J. M. B.   R

61st Divisional Orders.
May 1917.

                              Number 6.

DIVISIONAL ROUTINE ORDERS,
by
Major-General Colin Mackenzie. C.B.,
Commanding 61st Division.
--------oOo--------

Headquarters, 1st May, 1917.

1098. IMMEDIATE REWARDS.
In future, all immediate rewards will be published in Army Routine Orders.
A copy will be sent direct from Fourth Army Headquarters to each Officer, N.C.O., and man whose name is thus published.
It is understood that these awards are published in Brigade Routine Orders and in the orders of the Units concerned.

1099. DIVISIONAL SANITARY WORKSHOP.
Applications for articles to be made in the Divisional Sanitary Workshop are to be addressed to the O.C. 72nd Sanitary Section, AUNROIR.

1100. ESTIMATED CASUALTIES.
Reference D.R.O. 1074 dated 21/4/17.
The Estimated Casualty phase which started on night 21st/22nd April will now close, and a new phase will start from midnight 30th April/1st May.
Units reporting any Estimated Casualties after this date will not include those submitted before 30th April/1st May.

1101. SANITATION.
Sick Wastage would be greatly reduced if more attention was paid to Army Routine Order 846.
It is essential that units should ensure that this order is obeyed in every respect.

1102. FUEL.
Issues of fuel at Winter scale will cease from 30th April, 1917.

1103. VENEREAL.
It has been ascertained that many men are unaware of the dangers of venereal disease in AMIENS.
Orders are, therefore, to be issued by all units warning the troops of the dangers of intercourse with prostitutes.

1104. FIELD CASHIER.
Until further notice the Field Cashier will visit Divisional Headquarters on Mondays and Thursdays each week from 2-30.p.m. to 4-30.p.m.

1105. TRANSPORT ROUTES.
Owing to constant enemy shelling of the SAVY - HOLNON road, all transport from ETREILLERS to HOLNON will proceed via ATTILLY, and not through SAVY.

H.C. Singleton
Lieut-Colonel.
A.A. & Q.M.G.,
61st Division.

To L/By Midland.   File in Divisional Orders Cover.

DIVISIONAL ROUTINE ORDERS
by
Major-General Colin Mackenzie, C.B.,
Commanding 61st Division.
- - - - - -oOo- - - - - -

Headquarters, 2nd May, 1917.

1106...EMPTY OIL DRUMS:

The percentage of oil drums returned to the base is not satisfactory.

It has been notified by Fourth Army Headquarters that, unless a large increase in the percentage of emptied returned to the base is shewn in the near future, it will become necessary to apply the same regulations to oil drums as has been applied to 2 gallon petrol tins.

See D.R.O's 980 of March 19th, 1917, and 1011 of April 3rd, 1917.

[signature]
D.A.A.G
Lieut-Colonel,
A.A.&.Q.M.G., 61st Division.

NOTICE.

LOST:- last week between GERMAINE and VAUX a pair of
Field Glasses, - No. on glasses 27986,
Maker - Lemaire Fabr., PARIS.
If found please return to Town Major, GERMAINE.

File in Div. Orders

DIVISIONAL ROUTINE ORDERS
by
Major-General Colin Mackenzie, C.B.,
Commanding 61st Division.
- - - - - -oOo- - - - - -

Headquarters, 4th May, 1917.

1108... DIVINE SERVICE:
Services will be held on Sunday next, May 6th, in Church Room Divisional Headquarters, as under :-

CHURCH OF ENGLAND:
7-30 a.m. Holy Communion;
9-15 a.m. Service for Headquarters Staff;
10-0 a.m. Church Parade;
10-40 a.m. Holy Communion.

PRESBYTERIAN, WESLEYAN & UNITED BOARD:
11-15 a.m. Church Parade, followed by Holy Communion.

There will also be a joint Service for all above-named Denominations (C.of.E. and non-C.of.E.) at 6-30 p.m. in the Church Room.

1109... HONOURS AND AWARDS:
Under authority granted by His Majesty the King, the Field Marshal Commanding-in-Chief, has awarded decorations to the Officers and N.C.O. shown below :-

MILITARY CROSS:

| 2nd Lieut. J.P. WAYTE | 2/4th Bn. Oxford & Bucks L. I; |
| Captain C.Q.J. YOUNG, | 2/2nd (S.M.) Field Ambulance, R.A.M.C., (T.F.). |

DISTINGUISHED CONDUCT MEDAL:

No. 240,069 Corporal (L/Sgt.)
F. DAVIS ..... 2/5th Bn. Gloucester Regt.

MILITARY MEDAL:

Under authority granted by His Majesty the King (M.S.^{H} 2260 dated 2/6/16), the Corps Commander has awarded the MILITARY MEDAL to the undernamed :-

No. 24170, Sgt. O. HAWKINS,   184th Machine Gun Coy.,
                              M. G. Corps;
No. 266272 Cpl. A.E.WINDSOR   2/1st Bucks Bn.
                              Oxford & Bucks L.I;
No. 500568 2nd Cpl. H.T.MILLER
                              61st Div. Signal Coy., R.E., (T.F.),
                              182nd Bde. Section.

1110... DIVISIONAL DISBURSING OFFICER:
The instructions contained in Q.900 of the 3rd May re Divisional Disbursing Officer will be held in obeyance until further orders.

P. T. O.

1111...FIRES IN BARNS - PRECAUTIONARY MEASURES:

In many barns in the present area the flooring appears sound and solid but in reality is only the coating of dust and mud over, in many cases, three or four feet of straw -

This straw should be immediately removed outside the billet. -

Cases have arisen where, after the intense heat occasioned by the close packing of the straw, fermentation arises and when wind reaches the place, the straw at once breaks into flames.

1112...DISCIPLINE:

Cases have recently occurred of men not using latrines at night but fouling the ground in the neighbourhood of billets, cookhouses, wells, etc.

Severe disciplinary action should be taken against offenders in this respect.

H. C. Singleton
Lieut-Colonel,
A.A.&.Q.M.G., 61st Division.

N O T I C E:

PAY: All French Interpreters will report for pay at the French Mission office, AUROIR, on May 6th, 1917, at 10-0 a.m.

File in Div. Orders

DIVISIONAL ROUTINE ORDERS,
by
Major-General Colin Mackenzie, C.B.,
Commanding 61st Division.
————oOo————

Headquarters, 7th May, 1917.

1116. **HONOURS AND AWARDS.**

Under authority granted by His Majesty the King, the Field Marshal Commanding-in-Chief has awarded decorations to the officers shown below :-

DISTINGUISHED SERVICE ORDER. (Date of award 5-5-17).

Captain (A/Major) J. R. BARRY, R.F.A.
attached 307th Brigade. R.F.A. (T.F.).

BAR TO MILITARY CROSS. (Date of award 5-5-17).

Second Lieutenant (Temp.Lieut.) K. E. Brown, M.C.,
2/4th Bn. Oxfordshire & Buckinghamshire
Light Infantry. (T.F.).

MILITARY CROSS. (Date of award 5-5-17)

Lieutenant S. A. PAKEMAN,
4th Bn. Wiltshire Regiment, (T.F.)., attd.,
2/5th Bn. Gloucestershire Regiment. (T.F.).

1117. **SANITATION.**

Owing to the fly breeding season being now imminent, the provision in the area (including the trenches) of fly-proof latrines with automatically closing lids, has become a very urgent matter.

As the sanitary Section is unable to cope with all the requirements in this respect, battalion pioneers must take up the provision of these seats where required.

As a temporary measure, pending the provision of fly-proof latrines, shallow straddle trenches may be used, but the immediate covering of excreta must be insisted on. Less than one foot of earth over excreta will not infallibly prevent flies emerging from eggs which have been deposited before excreta is covered.

The provision of covered urine pits must not be lost sight of.

H. C. Singleton,
Lieut-Colonel.
A.A. & Q.M.G.,
61st Division.

NOTICE.

LOST: On night of 6th inst., between 61st Divisional Headquarters and MONCHY LAGACHE, (via BEAUVOIS and TERTRY) two side curtains for Wolseley Car. Information to A.P.M. 61st Division.

File.

DIVISIONAL ROUTINE ORDERS,
by
Major-General Colin Mackenzie. C. B.,
Commanding 61st Division.
---oOo---

Headquarters, 8th May, 1917.

1118. **HONOURS AND AWARDS.**
Under authority granted by His Majesty The King, (M.S.H. 2260 dated 2/6/16), the Corps Commander has awarded decorations to the following :-

MILITARY MEDAL. (Date of award 7-5-17).

No. 4847 L/Cpl. T.W.GREEN,	184 Company, M.G. Corps.
No. 201069 L/Cpl. A.E.SLOPER,	2/4th Bn. Oxford & Bucks L.I.
No. 200084 Sgt. G.W.BUTCHER,	do.

1119. **NUMBERING OF BILLETS.**
Units in conjunction with Town Majors will take steps to have the billeting accommodation of the villages in the Divisional area numbered, showing accommodation available in cellars and billets.

A return, together with a map will be rendered to this office not later than the 14th inst., by the Town Majors of FORESTE and AUROIR, and the Brigades in occupation of ATILLY, VAUX, ETREILLERS and SAVY, giving the above information.

1120. **REMOVAL OF MATERIAL FROM DAMAGED HOUSES.**
It is reported by the French authorities that much of the sound woodwork and brick walls in good condition are being removed and demolished by British Troops for use on roads and for other purposes.

All ranks therefore, are hereby ordered under no circumstances to remove sound woodwork or touch any bricks, (except those in walls which are in a dangerous condition or which have already fallen down), unless permission has been obtained from the Town Major, or other appointed Officer.

1121. **DELETION OF XI CORPS SIGN ON VEHICLES.**
Attention is directed to Divisional Routine Order 759 of 22-1-17, which has not been complied with in all cases.
These signs should be at once painted out.

1122. **REPLACEMENT OF EQUIPMENT, CLOTHING AND NECESSARIES.**
Attention is directed to Field Service Regulations, Part II, §76 §§ (4).
(1). Demands for replacement of these articles, when bona fide lost owing to the exigencies of the Service, will be countersigned by the O.C. the unit, to that effect.
(2) Demands for replacement of articles lost by negligence, and for which payment will be exacted from individuals, will bear a statement to that effect, signed by the O.C. the unit.
The price of articles, when not known, can be obtained from D.A.D.O.S.

Separate demands as at (1) and (2), must be rendered to D.A.D.O.S. who has to differentiate between such issues,

H. C. Singleton.

Lieut-Colonel.
A.A. & Q.M.G.,
61st Division.

File Div. Order Book

DIVISIONAL ROUTINE ORDERS
by
Major-General Colin Mackenzie, C.B.,
Commanding 61st Division.
- - - - - - oOo - - - - - -

Headquarters, 9th May, 1917.

1123. COURT OF INQUIRY:
Reference D.R.O. 883 of 3rd March, 1917.
The Court of Inquiry therein detailed will re-assemble at 11-30 a.m. on May 15th at the Infantry Brigade Headquarters in GERMAINE
The Court will be re-constituted as follows :-

PRESIDENT:
Colonel R.F. ANDERSON, Inspector of Fires.

MEMBERS:
Major A.B. WHITFIELD,   2/6th Warwicks;
Captain L.T.V. BARNES, 2/5th Warwicks.

Proceedings, in triplicate, will be forwarded to this office.
The G.O.C., 183 Infantry Brigade, will arrange for the attendance of necessary witnesses.

1124. FOOD - PROTECTION OF:
Many units in the division have not yet indented for butter muslin in accordance with Fourth Army R.O. 846 (SANITATION) of 16-4-1917.
Indents should be forwarded at once to A.D.M.S.

1125. PICKED UP NAILS:
A great number of horses are still being evacuated suffering from "picked up nails".
Every endeavour must be made to reduce this cause of wastage and it must be impressed on all ranks that it is their duty to remove, off the ground, any nails that they may come across.

1126. TRAFFIC ORDERS:
D.R.O. No. 1105 dated 1st May, 1917, is cancelled.
Revised traffic orders dated 8/5/17 are being issued to all concerned.

1127. DECAUVILLE TRUCKS - LOCATION:
If any decauville trucks are found lying about in divisional area unused, the location of these trucks should be sent to Div. H.Q., gauge of wheels and condition of trucks should also be stated.

1128. SURPLUS & DEFICIENT HORSE TRANSPORT RETURN:
Reference A.R.O. 939 dated 4/5/17.
This return will in future be rendered monthly, instead of weekly, by all units so as to reach this office on the last Wednesday in every month.

Lieut-Colonel,
A.A.&.Q.M.G., 61st Division.

File D.R.O. Cow

DIVISIONAL ROUTINE ORDERS,
by
Major-General Colin Mackenzie, C.B.,
Commanding 61st Division.
---oOo---

Headquarters, 11th May, 1917.

1131. **DIVINE SERVICE.**
Services will be held on Sunday next, May 13th, in Church Room, Divisional Headquarters, as under :-

CHURCH OF ENGLAND.

      7-30.a.m. Holy Communion.
      9-15.a.m. Service for Headquarters Staff.
      10-0. a.m. Church Parade.
      10-40.a.m. Holy Communion.

PRESBYTERIAN, WESLEYAN AND UNITED BOARD.

      11-15.a.m. Church Parade, followed by
      Holy Communion.

There will also be a joint Service for all above-named Denominations (C. of E. and non C. of E.), at 6-30.p.m. in the Church Room.

1132. **DISTINGUISHING MARKS.**
Divisional Routine Order No. 273 of 10-8-16, is cancelled. The distinguishing marks laid down therein will cease to be used.
The Armlets laid down in S.S. 135 Section XXXII, para. 2, (Training of Divisions for Offensive Actions), will be taken into use by the following :-

    Scouts and Snipers. . . . . Green Band.
    Runners. Red Band.
    Regimental and Company Signallers . . . . . . Blue Band.

These bands will be 1½ inches wide, and will be worn round the left forearm.
Material should be demanded from D.A.D.O.S.
Material for the other armlets described in the paragraph mentioned above, will be kept in store by D.A.D.O.S. for issue when necessity arises.

1133. **BATHING.**
Arrangements for bathing men at ETREILLERS, X.26.d.3.4. are now complete. Application should be made to the N.C.O. in charge.

1134. **FIRE PRECAUTIONS AT AMMUNITION DUMPS.**
Sand or fine earth will be kept at all ammunition dumps for dealing with an outbreak of fire.
Hay, Oats, or Petrol, must not be stored near any ammunition dump.

1135. **SALVAGE DUMPS OF AMMUNITION OR EXPLOSIVES.**
All salvage dumps of ammunition or explosives are to be kept entirely apart from other dumps.

                        Lieut-Colonel.
                        A.A. & Q.M.G.,
                        61st Division.

File in Divisional Routine Order Cover.

DIVISIONAL ROUTINE ORDERS
by
Major-General Colin Mackenzie, C.B.,
Commanding 61st Division.
- - - - - - oOo - - - - -

Headquarters, 12th May, 1917.

1136...**LEAVE - MEDICAL INSPECTION BEFORE DEPARTURE:**
Reference to A.R.O. No. 949 of 7th inst.
Men proceeding on leave should be medically inspected by Medical Officers of their unit for Scabies and Vermin. If the men are found to be free from both, a certificate should be given in accordance with A.R.O. 949.

1137...**BILLETING IN EVACUATED AREAS:**
In all cases of evacuated Towns where no Communal Authorities are present, the original and duplicate Billeting Certificates and Distribution Lists are to be sent to the O. i/c. Branch Requisition Office, Fourth Army.
In evacuated areas, it is essential that the conditions as laid down in S.S. 396, para.(i), page 13 should be borne in mind :-
"Billeting certificates will only be given for "accommodation which may reasonably be said to have been actually provided, e.g., certificates for billeting should not be given for such shelter as is obtainable in abandoned ruins.
The application of this instruction will be decided by Commanders on the spot, due regard being had to the quality of the accommodation provided.
The absence of owners will not "ipso facto" affect their right to receive any billeting monies to which they may be entitled."

1138...**TRAFFIC - ROUTES:**
FOURQUES BRIDGE at V.7. 0.3. is now opened to traffic up to 6 ton axle loads.

Lieut-Colonel,
A.A.&Q.M.G., 61st Division.

DRINKING WATER - CARE OF: (Third Army R.O. No. 756 dated 11-5-17).
All reservoirs containing drinking water for troops are to be covered as soon as practicable, after being installed, to prevent contamination from dust.
Reservoirs near roads and horse lines, and canvas tanks on the ground, should be dealt with first.
Adequate police arrangements at all water points must be arranged, and the practice of drawing water by dipping utensils into the tanks is forbidden.

THIRD ARMY SCHOOL OF COOKERY: (Third Army R.O. No. 757 dated 11-5-17).
The Army School of Cookery is now established at NOYELLE VION. All Staff, Commanding or other Officers are invited to visit the School any day between 9 a.m. and 5 p.m.

ROADS - UPKEEP OF: (C.R.O. 1940 dated 31-3-1917).
Although "Transportation" is responsible for the upkeep and repair of roads, Divisions are responsible that the roads in villages are kept clean, and that gutters and drains are cleared of accumulations of mud and water.

STOKES MORTAR 3-INCH: (C.R.O. 1970 dated 11-4-17).
In order to eliminate the causes of prematures with 3-inch Stokes Mortar, the following precautions will be taken :-
(a) The end of the Bickford fuze which is inserted into the detonator should not be cut on the slant.
(b) When the mouth of the detonator is being crimped on to the Bickford fuze, a space of at least a quarter of an inch must be left between the end of the fuze and the top of the fulminate.
(Authority :- Third Army 0/78/160 dated 8-4-17, VI Corps Q/2/74).

SMALL BOX RESPIRATOR: (C.R.O. 1972 dated 11-4-17).
Owing to the deposit of moisture on the inside of the eyepieces of Small Box Respirators after prolonged wearing, it is found necessary to provide anti-dimming composition for use with these appliances. A small 'outfit' consisting of a tube of anti-dimming composition and a soft cloth for applying it, together with instructions for use, the whole contained in a box of small size capable of being carried in the haversack of the respirator, has been designed and approved for issue.
Supplies of Small Box Respirators, complete with these outfits, are commencing to arrive in this country, and it is notified for information that all Small Box Respirators containing these outfits are marked "A.D.", and that the serial number of this first lot of respirators so fitted is No. 74.
Outfits for the respirators already in use are due from home and a further notification will be made when supplies are available.
(Authority:- Third Army 0/241 dated 10-4-17, VI Corps Q/8/32).

AREA STORES: (C.R.O. 1978 dated 12-4-17).
All Divisions on leaving VI Corps will return all Armstrong Huts, tents or shelters, which have been allotted to them while in this Corps.
Armstrong Huts will be handed over to the nearest Town Major. Tents and Shelters will be handed over to the Town Major of DUISANS or WARLUS.
A report will be sent by Divisions to Corps "Q", stating numbers handed over, and all Town Majors will also report numbers received.
Lorry tanks and G.S. Wagons fitted with water tanks, and extra water carts will be ordered to report to the Divisional Train of the relieving Division, and a report sent to Corps "Q" stating this has been done.
All Pack Saddlery will also be handed over to the relieving Division, and a statement of numbers so handed over will be sent by the outgoing Division to Corps Headquarters.
The extra belts for machine guns will also be handed over.
(VI Corps Q/66).

P. T. O.

- 4 -

ABANDONED VEHICLES: (C.R.O. 1983 dated 13-4-17).
Cases are occuring of vehicles being abandoned on the line of march owing to their breaking down.
The correct procedure in such cases is to leave a guard, but if this is impracticable for any reason, a wire should be sent to the Headquarters of the Corps in whose area the vehicle is abandoned, giving the map reference of the spot.
(VI Corps Q/850).

WATERING HORSES: (C.R.O. 1988 dated 14-4-17).
Losses in horses are due to various causes, the chief of which is debility.
Debility arises from various causes, the chief of which is lack of horsemastership.
Horsemastership includes watering horses and the supervision of the arrangements for watering horses is as a rule (especially in the Artillery) very bad. If horses do not get enough water to drink when doing hard work they rapidly become debilitated. There is plenty of water in the Corps area, and failure to ensure that horses are properly watered is entirely due to disregard of orders.
The following orders are to be implicity carried out :-
(i) Every Division will at once place a water guard, or water police, on all horse watering troughs in the Divisional area.
(ii) These guards are responsible for seeing that all troughs are full before the horses arrive to drink, that there is no over-crowding, that there is no waste of water, and that all breaches of watering orders are at once brought to notice.
(iii) It is absolutely forbidden that one man takes more than two horses to water.
(iv) It is absolutely forbidden that more horses are taken to water at troughs at one time than the length of trough permits.
(v) It is absolutely forbidden that all horses of a Battery proceed to water at the same time in one long string. Not more than 25 horses at a time, should as a rule, proceed to water at the same time. An interval of at least 100 yards should separate these groups.
(vi) An officer must invariably be sent with all Artillery watering parties. This officer must see that the troughs are full before allowing his horses to water.

The above orders are to be made known to all officers and N.C.Os. If there is a shortage of actual length of horse watering troughs provided by the Corps, or from civilian sources, then Divisions must make their own arrangements to increase the accommodation. As it is possible that we are entering on a period of moving warfare, in which the care of horseflesh is one of imperative necessity, then all concerned must learn that it is their duty to assist, so far as they are able, in keeping their animals in good condition by forethought, initiative and obedience to orders.
(VI Corps Q/423).

STOKES' SHELL CASES: (C.R.O. 1994 dated 16-4-17).
Cases packing Stokes 3" Shell H.E. are urgently required at the Base for repacking salvaged shells returned from Railheads.
Every endeavour should be made to recover as many as possible in good condition and return them to Railhead.
(Authority:- Third Army C/36/4, dated 15-4-17. VI Corps Q/1/90).

DIVISIONAL ROUTINE ORDERS,
by
Major-General Colin Mackenzie, C.B.,
Commanding 61st Division.
--------oOo--------

Headquarters, 23rd May, 1917.

1151. **FIRES IN DUG-OUTS.**
General Routine Order No. 2310 dated 20th May, 1917, is republished for information.

"Several lives were recently lost through a fire in dug-outs. The following instructions will be observed in future:-

(a) Petrol will on no account be used to replace paraffin in Primus or in any other heating or cooking stoves.

(b) Paraffin, petrol, oil and candles will be stored in a special dug-out away from all fires.

(c) All receptacles containing petrol will be marked PETROL in large distinctive letters.

(d) Candles and fires are never to be left burning when dug-outs are unoccupied.

(e) The portion of the wall and floor of all dug-outs in contact with braziers or stoves will be lined with tin, or with corrugated iron.

(f) Underground cook-houses will be provided with a door covered with tin, and a number of filled sandbags will be kept in a suitable position, so that, when a fire breaks out, the doors can be shut and a barricade of sandbags rapidly constructed to isolate the fire. A bucket of sand will be kept near each cook-house to extinguish small fires.

(g) When a fire breaks out underground, the N.C.O., or man responsible for giving warning, will clear everyone at once out of the whole system, sending the men out in one direction, if possible away from the fire. As the fumes are poisonous and far reaching in their effects, the entrances and trenches in their vicinity must also be kept clear of men.

(h) Men must not wait to put on equipment.

(i) In extensive dug-out systems, isolation doors, with handy stores of sandbags on each side of them, will be constructed at suitable points.

(k) If a Mine Rescue Station is situated in the vicinity, a notice should be posted in all dug-out systems showing its position. The men on duty at the Station are available to render assistance in rescuing men and extinguishing the fire.

(l) Security is best assured by holding frequent fire drills."

H. C. Singleton.

Lieut-Colonel.
A.A. & Q.M.G.,
61st Division.

NOTICE.

PAY: All French Interpreters will report for pay at the French Mission on or before the 25th inst.

DIVISIONAL ROUTINE ORDERS
by
Major-General Colin Mackenzie, C.B.,
Commanding 61st Division.

- - - - - oOo - - - - - -

Headquarters, 25th May, 1917.

1152...**DIVINE SERVICE:**
Services C. of E. will be held on Sunday, May 27th, (Whit Sunday) as follows :-
        8-0 a.m.   Holy Communion;
       10-0 a.m.   Church Parade;
       10-40 a.m. Holy Communion;
       6-30 p.m.   Evening Service;
All services will be held in C.A. Hut, on cross-roads, WARLUS.

1153...**FOURTH ARMY STANDING ORDERS:**
All copies of Fourth Army Standing Orders in possession of units of the Division will be returned so as to reach this office by 29th.inst.

1154...**CANTEEN:**
The 61st Division Canteen will open at BERNEVILLE to-morrow May 26th.

1155...**CARE OF AMMUNITION & OTHER INFLAMMABLE MATERIAL:**
In accordance with VI Corps Routine Order No. 2201 dated 24th May, 1917, Third Army Routine Order No. 777 dated 21-5-1917, is re-published for information :-

" 1.   Fire, smoking or naked lights are forbidden within 200 yards of any dump or building where ammunition, petrol, explosives or other highly inflammable material of any kind are stored.

   2.   Drivers of lorries or other vehicles containing ammunition, explosives, petrol, etc., are not to smoke, or to allow naked lights or fires in such vehicles.

   3.   Every dump or building in which ammunition, explosives, petrol, etc., are stored will be in charge of an armed guard which will be visited and inspected by an officer by day and night.

   4.   The guard will not live in the dump or building, but permanent sentries must be posted thereon.

   5.   The officer in charge of the dump or building is responsible that application is made in writing to the proper authority to provide a guard of sufficient strength.

   6.   At every dump or building containing ammunition, explosives, petrol, etc., notice boards will be freely displayed, so that they cannot fail to attract attention, in letters four inches high - the word DANGER in red, thus :-

```
+-----------+
| DANGER.   |
| NO SMOKING|
| NO FIRES. |
+-----------+
```

Paras. 1 and 2 above will be read daily to all labour parties, guards, and lorry drivers employed at dumps or buildings containing ammunition, explosives, petrol, etc. "

This order will be repeated in the orders of all Divisions and Corps Heavy Artillery.

1156. **SUPPLY COLUMN WORKSHOPS:**
The 61st Supply Column Workshops are situated near DAINVILLE at L.30.c.6.9. (Sheet 51 c.).

(P. T. O.

1157... ORDNANCE:
Divisional Ordnance Stores are situated at WARLUS at K.36.c.5.9., (Sheet 51 c.).

1158... THIRD ARMY ROUTINE ORDERS:
The following Third Army Routine Orders are republished for information and guidance :-

DISCIPLINE - (A.R.O. 311):
1. Purchase & Sale of Spirits or Alcoholic Drinks.
Beer, cider and the ordinary light wines are the only form of alcoholic drinks which may be bought or accepted by the troops at any kind of hotel, estaminet, shop or private house.
The Sale, purchase, or acceptance, of spirits or liquers of any kind is forbidden.
2. Taking of Alcoholic Drink to billets.
N.C.Os. and men are forbidden to take beer or any form of alcoholic drink to their billet.
3. Regimental Canteens:
Beer may be bought for supplying Regimental Canteens, but the hours for the sale of the beer or other form of alcoholic drink in these canteens must not be different from those laid down for estaminets in G.R.O. 1107, viz :- 11 a.m. to 1 p.m. and 6 p.m. to 8 p.m. At other times the canteen may be used as a recreation room.

HOTELS - (A.R.O. 436):
Hotels in Third Army area close at 9-15 p.m., and the proprietors of any which remain open after that hour are liable to prosecution. Officers proceeding on, or returning from, leave, etc., cannot, therefore, obtain dinner after that time. All Officers dining at Hotels in the area must leave the premises by 9-15 p.m. unless they occupy a room in the hotel for the night.

SALE OF ALCOHOL - (A.R.O. 451).
With reference to Third Army Routine Order 311 dated 21st February, 1916, it is to be understood that officers are included in the prohibition regarding the purchase of alcoholic drinks, other than beer, cider and light wines, at Hotels, Cafes, etc., in the Third Army area.
This order is to be re-published by all units in their Regimental or Corps orders.

STEEL HELMETS - (A.R.O. 480):
Men have been noticed wearing the lining of their steel helmets as a cap. This practice is to cease forthwith. It is forbidden to remove the lining from the steel helmet.

STEEL HELMETS: - (A.R.O. 541):
Army Routine Order No. 339 is cancelled, and the following substituted :-
1. Steel helmets will be worn at all times by all ranks engaged in operations.
2. When troops are not engaged in operations, steel helmets will be worn by all ranks on guard, on parade, when training, or on the march.

ACCIDENTAL INJURIES - (A.R.O. 241):
With reference to A.R.O. 190, cases still occur of men accidentally wounding themselves by tampering with detonators, fuzes, cartridges, grenades, bombs and shells which they have found.
N.C.O's and men finding such articles must not tamper with them in any way.
Small articles such as detonators, fuzes and cartridges, should be handled with care and taken to an Officer as early as possible; bombs and shells should not be touched, but their position reported to an Officer, so that steps may be taken by the Royal Engineers to destroy them or render them harmless. All Officers should be instructed in the method of removing and disposing of unexploded grenades.

(Cont'd.

grenades/

The retention of any such articles as trophies is prohibited.

In future, any N.C.O. or man who injures himself through neglect to comply with the above order will be tried by Court-Martial.

This order is to be read out on three consecutive Battery, squadron, or company parades.

EXPLOSIONS - INSTRUCTIONS RE - (A.R.O. 380):
(1) It is to be impressed upon all ranks that shells that have been fired, or grenades or bombs that have been thrown, and that have failed to explode, are always dangerous, and may explode at any time.
(2) When blind shells, bombs, grenades, or any explosives are found, whether of German, French or British manufacture, N.C.Os and men are forbidden to touch them. Their position is to be reported to an Officer so that steps may be taken to destroy them or render them harmless.
(3) The retention of the above-mentioned articles or any other explosives as trophies is prohibited.
(4) Grenades thrown for instruction which fail to explode, are not to be touched except by the Officer in charge of the instruction, who will be held personally responsible that every precaution possible is taken to avoid accident to himself and others.
(5) Special grenades will be set apart in all units and schools for instructional use. These grenades are not to be fitted with detonators and thrown as "live". Only new grenades that have not been tampered with in any way are to be used for "live" practice.
(6) When "live" grenades are thrown for practice, all men near are to be under cover, and men throwing the grenades are to be in a trench deep enough to give them complete cover, or behind a splinter proof barricade not less than six feet high.
(7) Any N.C.O. or man who injures himself, or causes injury to another, by disobeying any of the foregoing instructions, will be tried by Court-Martial.
(8) Every accident due to faulty ammunition, disobedience of these orders, lack of supervision or carelessness, will form the subject of a Court of Enquiry.

If the accident is thought to be due to a fault in our own Ammunition, the I.O.O. Third Army, will be applied for to attend the Court. His address is I.O.O. H.Q., Third Army.

DISCIPLINE - (A.R.O. 148):
Reports have been received that some soldiers, when proceeding on leave, arrive BOULOGNE under the influence of drink.

In future, any soldier found in this condition, or found in possession of wine or spirits, either on arrival at the Port, or on the way to the Port, will be returned to his unit under escort and forfeit leave for six months.

This order is to be brought to the notice of all men before proceeding on leave.

AMMUNITION - MEN PROCEEDING ON LEAVE - (A.R.O. 226):
As, in spite of many warnings on this subject, N.C.O's and men continue to take their ammunition with them when proceedings on leave, any man found in possession of ammunition at the port of embarkation on, or after, 1st January, 1916, when about to proceed on leave, will be refused his leave and returned to his unit.

The Inspector-General of Communications has been requested to give effect to this order.

DISCIPLINE - ARTICLES THROWN FROM THE LEAVE TRAIN: -(A.R.O. 318):
It is forbidden to throw bottles and other articles from leave trains, as it is a danger to the railway employees working on the line.

This order should be brought to the notice of all men proceeding on leave.

MARCH DISCIPLINE - (A.R.O. 229):
A mounted N.C.O. must invariably ride in rear of any column of horsed transport to ensure march discipline being maintained and to see that the road is cleared when necessity demands that lorries or cars should pass.

HORSES: - (A.R.O. 378):
Government animals are constantly left in charge of civilian boys outside shops and houses in towns and villages in the Third Army Area.
This practice is forbidden.
Commanding Officers are directed to take disciplinary action in all cases where it is proved that Government animals have been left by those responsible for them in charge of civilians.

ORDERS FOR WATERING ANIMALS - (A.R.O. 390):
Owing to the lack of system which prevails in many units in the watering arrangements, the following routine will be observed :-
Animals will be paraded for watering not less than three times daily. One man will not be in charge of more than two animals. An Officer is to be present all the time; only in the event of no Officer being available may a senior N.C.O. be in charge.
When watering at troughs, a pumping party will be detailed to clean and fill the troughs before the first batch arrives and keeps them full until the parade is finished.
The Officer or N.C.O. in charge is responsible that the troughs are properly filled and kept full.
Animals are not to be crowded while drinking. They must not be closer together than one horse or mule to each four feet of trough.
Girths will be loosened and bits removed. Each batch will be kept at the water until all animals in the batch have finished drinking.

TOWN OF ARRAS - (A.R.O. 375):
The town of Arras is out of bounds to all ranks unless on duty.
Officers and other ranks entering the town on duty must be provided with a written pass signed by a Commanding or Staff Officer specifying the nature of the duty on which employed.
This does not apply to :-
                Staff Officers;
                Despatch riders;
                Orderlies with messages.

DISCIPLINE - (A.R.O. 457):
Before cleaning any part of a rifle, the magazine will invariably be removed and the bolt opened. This order is to be republished in the Regimental Orders of all units.

COURTS-MARTIAL - (A.R.O. 495):
Several cases have occurred recently where men who were under arrest in Field Ambulances or Casualty Clearing Stations in connection with self-inflicted wounds have been tried by Court-Martial and found "Not Guilty", but the finding of the Court has not been intimated to the Medical Authorities concerned
In such cases the Medical Authorities should always be informed immediately by the Officer Commanding the man's unit of the finding of "Not Guilty" in order that he may be released from arrest.

FIRES - (A.R.O. 449):
General Routine Orders 1295 and 1436 will be read out on parade to every unit at least once a month Officers Commanding units are held responsible that all Officers and men under their command are acquainted with these orders.

(Continued)

LEAKAGE OF MILITARY INFORMATION – (A.R.O. 488):
(i) With reference to Army Order dated 24th July, 1916, on the subject of LEAKAGE OF MILITARY INFORMATION: in every unit a book is to be kept in which this order will be pasted, and a nominal roll of the whole of the Officers in that unit entered in the book.
(ii) All Officers are to initial this book as having read the above mentioned Army Order on the 1st of every month, and each fresh Officer who arrives to join the unit will sign the book the day he joins.
(iii) These books will be inspected from time to time as the G.O.C., Third Army, may direct.

Lieut-Colonel,
A.A.&Q.M.G., 61st Division.

NOTICE:

THEATRE PARTY:
The 61st Division-"FROLICS" will open at DUISANS to-morrow, May 26th.
Performance will commence at 6-30 p.m. each evenin

DIVISIONAL ROUTINE ORDERS
by
Major-General Colin Mackenzie, C.B.,
Commanding 61st Division.
----- oOo -----

Headquarters, 26th May, 1917.

1159... **VI CORPS ROUTINE ORDERS:**
The following VI Corps Routine Orders have been republished as an Addendum to Divisional Orders of this date, for information and guidance:-
1957; 1975; 1977; 1982; 1986; 1987; 2005; 2006; 2029; 2034; 2048; 2050; 2051; 2064; 2065; 2071; 2073; 2079; 2083; 2096; 2097; 2105; 2109; 2131; 2135; 2148; 2164 and 2176.

1160... **WATER PURIFYING TABLETS:**
Any water purifying tablets which may be in the possession of individuals will be collected and returned to the S.S.O.

1161... **DIVINE SERVICE, May 27th, WHITSUNDAY:**
The 10 a.m. Parade Service will be in grounds of Corps Rest Station, opposite D.H.Q., and not in Church Army Hut.
The following services will be held in addition to those already announced:-
C. of E.,
9-15 a.m. Service for H.Q. Staff in "Q" Office.
Presbyterian, Wesleyan, etc.,
11-15 a.m. Service followed by Holy Communion, in C. A. Hut.
The 6-30 p.m. Service will be for all Denominations, as usual.

1162... **RAILWAY MATERIAL, etc., (FRENCH):**
No French railway property such as cranes and signal posts is to be interfered with or removed without reference to Army H.Q.

1163... **CASUALTY RETURNS:**
In future the daily Casualty wire will be sent so as to reach this office by 9 a.m., reporting actual casualties which have occurred for the 24 hours ending the previous mid-night.
Para. 7 of this office Q 44 dated 1-4-17 will be amended accordingly.
Estimated casualty wires will continue to be rendered as laid down in this office Q 44 dated 1st April, 1917.

E.P. Blenerne Major D?
for
Lieut-Colonel,
A.A.&.Q.M.G., 61st Division.

EXTRACTS FROM VI CORPS ROUTINE ORDERS:

(REPUBLISHED AS AN ADDENDUM TO 61st DIVISIONAL ROUTINE ORDERS No.1159 dated 26-5-1917).

HORSES AND MULES - BURIAL OF - (C.R.O. 1957 dated 5-4-17).

In the event of a horse or mule dying outside the area occupied by the unit to which it belongs, the unit nearest to the place where the dead animal is left will be held responsible that it is buried without loss of time.

Military Police will report to Divisional Headquarters or Corps Heavy Artillery any cases they may note.

WATER SUPPLY - POLICING OF - (C.R.O. 1975 dated 12-4-17).

Whenever a Division takes over any area in which there is any water point, arrangements are to be at once made to police the various water appliances, such as horse troughs, pumps, water cart refilling points and water bottle filling taps. The duties of the Water Police are to prevent overcrowding, waste of water and damage to material. The Police will also see that the troughs are kept full. Water points and police instructions are to be handed over from one Division to another on relief.

Attention is called to the want of supervision by officers of horse watering arrangements.

SANITATION - (C.R.O. 1977 dated 12-4-17).

All units occupying fresh ground are responsible that all necessary sanitary arrangements are put in hand as soon as the troops arrive on the ground, i.e. latrines must be prepared and refuse pits dug without waiting for orders from some higher authority. The Transport Lines of all Divisions require immediate attention in this respect.

LOOTING THE DEAD - (C.R.O. 1982 dated 13-4-17).

The attention of all concerned is to be directed to the fact that any man found in the act of "Looting the Dead" is liable to suffer death by being shot, and that no cases of this nature will be leniently dealt with.

ELECTRIC LIGHT PLANT - (C.R.O. 1986 dated 14-4-17).

Complaints have been received that unauthorised persons are interfering with the electric light plant in ARRAS, and are in some instances tapping the wires to obtain extensions of the system.

This practice will immediately cease, and any offenders will be severely dealt with.

CUTTING OF WOOD - (C.R.O. 1987 dated 14-4-17.).

No timber will be cut and no arrangements made with proprietors to cut timber excepting through the Forest Control Officers of the Army. These officers will make all necessary arrangements with owners and allot coupes for the cutting of fuel or other wood as required.

(Authority: - Q.M.G. 10015/12 (Q.A.2) dated 6-4-17, VI Corps A/3647).

TRAFFIC CONTROL - (C.R.O. 2006 dated 21-4-1917).

It is noticed that many troops, when halted for a short time on roads, during a block, remain in "Column of Route", standing easy in "fours". Unless it is perfectly certain that the block is only momentary, men should be made to form "two deep", or fall out, so as not to block traffic on the other portion of the road.

(P. T. O.)

SANITATION - (C.R.O. 2005 dated 21-4-17).
Now that some forward movement has taken place, and the ordinary routine of trench life has been to a certain extent, abandoned, it has become evident that the majority of the men have not been instructed in the ordinary principles of Sanitation. The ground is being fouled in every direction. Shell holes are being used as latrines and the excreta is not covered up.

Nearly every man is in possession of an intrenching implement or can get a spade. It must be at once impressed on every man that all excreta is to be covered over with earth. If no spade is available, earth can be kicked over the spot.

Refuse of all kinds, and empty tins, must be placed in shell holes, and covered over with earth. It is not sufficient to merely throw the refuse into holes and leave it there.

The above simple rules of sanitation are to be at once instilled into the minds of everybody. Partly disciplined troops, such as Labour Battalions, Army Troops, etc., are especially bad in sanitary matters.

If the above orders are not carried out, there will be outbreaks of disease, and myriads of flies everywhere, as soon as warm weather commences.

The above instructions are to be repeated in all Divisional and other orders.

SANITATION - (C.R.O. 2029 dated 26-4-17).
Corps Routine Order No. 2005 dated 21-4-1917, is not being obeyed. The areas near gun positions and Artillery horse lines are still being fouled. Little or no attention is being paid to sanitation or digging latrines.

Every Unit in the area East of ARRAS up to the actual fighting line, and including all Artillery positions, will at once set one or two men to work with spades covering up the filth in the shell holes. These men are also to dig proper latrines.

This order is to be re-published in all Divisional and unit orders.

IDENTITY DISCS - C.R.O. 2034 dated 27-4-17).
It is to be brought to the notice of all ranks that under no circumstances whatever is anybody to remove an identity disc or "small book" from a fallen comrade, unless he is a member of a burial party.

A few cases have occurred in the past, which have rendered identification of the body impossible.

FIELD CASHIER, VI CORPS - (C.R.O. 2048 dated 30-4-17).
The following programme of the Field Cashier, VI Corps, will come into operation on Wednesday, 2nd May, 1917 :-
Daily   ARRAS,   9 a.m. to 12-30 p.m;
                             2-30 p.m. to 6 p.m.
Wednesdays & Saturdays: DUISANS   9-30 to 11 a.m.
                WARLUS   12 noon to 1 p.m.
                BERNEVILLE   2-30 to 4 p.m.
                SIMENCOURT   4-30 to 6 p.m.
Note:- The office of the Field Cashier is at 6, Rue Jeanne d'ARC ARRAS.

SALVAGE - (C.R.O. 2051 dated 30-4-17).
The number of articles left in billets and in the streets of villages, by units is still enormous. As this wastage and loss can only occur through want of discipline and general slackness on the part of officers and men concerned, it will become necessary, if no improvement takes place at once, to publish the list of articles left behind, with the name of the unit which leaves them.

Gun ammunition is dropped alongside every road in the Corps area, and is even found lying about in villages a long way behind the firing line. Artillery Officers must have noticed these rounds lying about, but no action is ever taken to have them removed until a Staff Officer notices them and orders their removal.

In future, if loose rounds are found lying about, an Artillery Officer of the nearest formation will be ordered to see to their removal.

(Continued)

TRAFFIC - (C.R.O. 2050 dated 30-4-1917).
Empty motor lorries returning to ARRAS along the CAMBRAI Road are not to proceed at a greater rate than 6 miles per hour.
The Military Police are to strictly enforce this order.

ARRAS - (C.R.O. 2064 dated 3-5-17).
Owing to the fact that ARRAS has been full of troops of many Divisions who have only passed through and made no long stay, the town has now got into a most insanitary condition, and unless Divisions and detached units take this matter in hand, there may possibly be serious outbreaks of disease.

So far as the VI Corps is concerned, the town of ARRAS is divided into two areas, "A" and "B", each of which may contain one or more Brigades.

Any small or detached unit which may be billeted in either of those areas will be under the orders of the senior officer in each area.

The following orders are to be strictly carried out :-
(a) No horse lines are allowed in ARRAS except those of Divisional H.Q., Infantry Brigade H.Q., and Divisional Artillery H.Q.
(b) All units are to remove manure from their own transport to the manure dumps at G.20.a.1.1. or G.22.b.7.6. daily.
(c) All units are to remove dead horses to open land quite clear of the town, and bury them deep, first opening the carcase. At least four feet of earth must cover the carcase.
(d) All units are to clear out the refuse which has accumulated in the back premises of billets, and cart it in their own transport to the incinerators at G.26.d.8.9., G.22.b.6.3., or G.21.b.5.8.
(e) All units which have manure dumps, dead horses or heaps of refuse lying near their lines, are to dispose of them as above, whether they are responsible for the nuisance or not.
(f) Officers of units are to inspect their billets every day, and do their best to detect and punish men damaging or removing the property of the inhabitants. Officer's servants are often offenders in this respect.
(g) A.P.M's will get into touch with the A.P.M., ARRAS, and assist him with any police available.
(h) Units are to place Regimental Police over taps used for washing purposes, to prevent waste of water, and will report leaky pipes, etc., to the S.O., R.E., at the Town Commandant's office.
(j) Units are to provide receptacles for refuse at specified places near the entrance of their billets, whence their own transport can remove it.
(k) Units are to report to the Sanitary Officer, Town Commandant's Office, ARRAS, places where latrine buckets require emptying.
(l) Units are to provide parties to clean up the roads opposite their billets and cart the mud or dust to the mud dump at G.21 a.4.5. Units can obtain brooms for the purpose from the D.A.D.O.S.
(m) Units are to keep fire picquets ready to turn out in case of fire in the neighbourhood.
(n) Patrolling picquets will be provided as laid down in para. ii, Town Routine Order No. 2, dated 22nd April, 1917, to assist in the maintenance of order.
(o) Units are to provide N.C.Os. on duty at the Estaminets used by their men.
(p) Units will provide working parties and wagons to assist the Town Sanitary Officer as required.
(q) Units will give Area Assistant Town Majors early warning of any moves into or out of the Corps Areas in ARRAS.
(r) Divisions and units must indent for such disinfectants as they require.

(P. T. O.).

KITS OF DECEASED AND WOUNDED OFFICERS - DISPOSAL OF) (C.R.O. 2065
                                                     dated 3-5-17).
    Complaints appear at times in newspapers that articles have been
taken from deceased and wounded officers' kits in transit to England.
Very clear and definite orders have been issued as to how kits are to
be secured and sealed before being handed in to Railhead, and it has
been brought to notice that the reason why some kits may become
opened and possibly the contents lost or stolen, is because the kits
are not properly packed and sealed by units before they are sent to
Railhead.
    The instructions contained in C.R.Os. 1387 and 1830 are to be
carried out in detail. If they are not, then the blame for any
articles being lost or stolen rests with the unit which does not obey
orders.

LEAVE TO PARIS - (C.R.O. 2071 dated 4-5-17).
    Officers are permitted to proceed to PARIS on leave under the
following conditions :-
    (a) All applications must be submitted to Corps Headquarters
         for approval.
    (b) The number of applications must be strictly limited.
    (c) A sufficient reason should be given why the application is
         forwarded.
    (d) This leave is not in any way to be looked upon as a right.

NIGHT TRAFFIC - (C.R.O. 2073 dated 4-5-17).
    All lorries approaching ARRAS whether moving singly or in convoys
will extinguish their side lights at the following places :-
         DAINVILLE Station;
         Eastern exit of DAINVILLE Village;
         DECAUVILLE level crossing at G.13.d.2.4.
              (VI Corps :- A.89/9.).

SANITATION - (C.R.O. 2079 dated 5-5-17).
    The Manure Dump at G.20.d.7.2., just West of ARRAS, is not to be
used any more. A new dump is to be started at G.20.a.1.1., where
manure is to be placed in the ditch and burnt.
    This new dump will be under the supervision of the Sanitary Officer
in charge of ARRAS, who will arrange for the dump to be burnt or
treated with disinfectants according to the weather.
    Where units cannot make use of large dumps, they must make their
own arrangements for the disposal of manure, and must burn or
disinfect it. Disused trenches must be used in the forward area where
it is not desirable to have dumps always burning, and the manure
placed in these trenches must be covered over with earth or chalk.
    Trenches can also be used for purposes of burning manure, Salved
iron pickets should be laid across the trenches and the manure piled
on the top and burnt.

CORRESPONDENCE FOR SOLDIERS WHO HAVE BECOME CASUALTIES - (C.R.O. 2083
                                                     dated 6-5-17).
    Undeliverable correspondence for wounded soldiers should not be
redirected to the Field Ambulance or Casualty Clearing Station to
which it is supposed the soldier has been evacuated, but should be
endorsed "Hospital" or "Wounded", and returned to the Field Post Office.
    If the addressee is deceased or missing, the correspondence should
be so endorsed, the endorsement being signed by an officer, giving his
rank.
    Correspondence for soldiers who are sick should continue to be
redirected to a Field Ambulance, Casualty Clearing Station, or Hospital,
if the address is definitely known to the Post Orderly.
    This order is to be re-published in Unit Orders.

                                              (Continued.

SANITATION
(C.R.O. 2096 dated 8-5-17).

The Sanitary Officer in charge of ARRAS states :-
"The chief difficulty experienced in this area is the lack of systematic inspection of billets by officers quartered in the town. Most of the cookhouses have obviously never been inspected by an officer or N.C.O., and this is also true of the majority of billets".

Numerous orders on this subject have already been issued by the Corps, and if Divisions and detached units cannot effect an improvement by means of efficient supervision and discipline then it will become necessary to pillory the offending Divisions and detached units in Corps Routine Orders.

KITS OF DECEASED AND WOUNDED OFFICERS - DISPOSAL OF - (C.R.O. 2097 dated 8-5-17).

With reference to para. 2 of Corps Routine Order No. 2065, dated 3-5-17, the instructions contained in General Routine Orders Nos. 1387 and 1820 are to be carried out in detail, otherwise kits will not be accepted at Railhead.

ANTI-GAS APPLIANCES - CARE OF - (C.R.O. 2105 dated 9-5-17).

Cases have occurred of articles such as knives, forks, etc., being carried in the satchels of box respirators. This eventually ends in the mask being perforated and rendered useless.

Officers Commanding Units will take steps to satisfy themselves that nothing is carried in the satchel except the respirator.

MARCH DISCIPLINE - (C.R.O. 2109 dated 10-5-17).

It is reported that troops have marched over the aerodrome at WAGNONLIEU, thus interfering with the landing of machines.

Troops are not to trespass on aerodromes.

SANITATION - (C.R.O. 2131 dated 13-5-17).

The idea appears to have grown up in certain Divisions and amongst Corps Troops that because there are Sanitary Sections, therefore no unit need take any trouble to keep their own areas clean. This idea is absolutely incorrect.

Medical Officers in charge of units are also to blame, as it is quite evident that they do not all daily go round the billets and areas occupied by the units which they have in their medical charge.

The Field Service Regulations on the subject are perfectly clear, and have not been altered since the war began.

Field Service Regulations, Part II, Sections 82, 83, 84 and 85, contain full instructions for everybody, and are to be carried out.

The duties of Regimental officers as regards sanitation are definitely laid down in these sections, which amongst other things say :-

(1) "The commander of every unit & formation is responsible for the sanitary condition of the quarters or localities occupied by his command, and for taking all measures necessary for the preservation of the health of those under him. He is also responsible for seeing that each officer and soldier observes all sanitary orders, and for the good order and cleanliness of that portion of qa quarter or locality under his charge, irrespective of the period for which it may be occup -ied."

(2) "The sanitary service of field units is organized upon the principle that every unit, through its commander, is responsible for its own sanitation and for the sanitary condition of any area which it may occupy. For this purpose each unit is provided with a regimental sanitary detachment, as shown in War Establishments.

The medical officer of a unit is responsible to its commander for the efficient performance of the work of the regimental sanitary detachment.

(P. T. O.)

CASUALTIES IN ARRAS - (C.R.O. 2135 dated 14-5-17).
In addition to, and quite apart from, casualty wires forwarded through the usual channels, the senior officer of a unit, or detachment quartered in ARRAS will report to the Town Commandant, ARRAS, daily by 12 noon, VIA the Division by which the unit or detachment is administered, the numbers of officers and other ranks killed or wounded within the boundary of the town during the 24 hours ended the previous mid-night.

Officers in charge of units or detachments not administered by a division will render the report direct to Town Commandant.
The reports will be made on the following form :-
(UNIT or DETACHMENT):

....
Attached to or belonging to ..... Corps.
_____

Casualties within the boundaries of ARRAS during 24 hours ended 12 midnight .... / .... (month) 1917.
_____

Officers ....killed ....wounded.
Others ....killed ....wounded.

..........1917. ....Signature.
_____

Nill returns are not required.

SANITATION - (C.R.O. 2148 dated 16-5-17).
Much more can be done to improve the bivouac sites and horse lines of all units in the Corps area round ARRAS, and especially to the East and South East.
Every unit should fill in a few shell holes daily and remove iron and wooden stakes and wire, and should fill in dismantled, unused trenches. Short lengths of trench should be set apart daily as refuse pits, and the trench filled in next day and be well rammed.
All wooden pickets should be collected, and those which are broken or rotting can be used as firewood. Iron pickets of all descriptions are to be collected and taken to the nearest R.E. or Salvage Dump.
Barbed wire should be disentangled, being cut for the purpose into short lengths, if necessary, and rolled up on pickets. French wire, when the connecting wire has been cut, can be rolled or coiled up. All will be returned to the R.E. or Salvage Dump.
If units carry out the above instructions daily and systematically not only will clear level camping grounds be available for all concerned, but horses will be saved many injuries from barbed wire. The policy at present carried out by many units of sitting down and doing nothing at all to improve the ground is to cease.
Definite defence lines, properly wired, such as the Corps lines, are of course not to be touched until further orders.
The above orders are to be repeated in all Divisional and unit orders.
(VI Corps C/964.).

SANITATION - (C.R.O. 2164 dated 18-5-17).
(i) Horses are not to be stabled or picketed in any of the houses of ST.SAUVEUR or RONVILLE, or in the back yards or orchards of these places.
(ii) A manure dump has been started at M.5.b.6.6. for transport lines in the area between RONVILLE and ACHICOURT. The O.C. 3.a. Sanitary Section will arrange for supervision and control of this dump. Units are responsible for bringing all manure not immediately buried in disused trenches, and depositing it in accordance with the instructions of the N.C.O. in charge.

(C o n t i n u e d)

WATER and SANITATION - (C.R.O. 2176 dated 18 19th May, 1917).

It has been brought to notice that men are in the habit of taking water out of reservoirs by means of pails and various types of drinking vessels. This practice is absolutely forbidden.

It is also forbidden to wash up vehicles or dump refuse anywhere close to water points, within 50 yards.

The forward water supply will be divided into three areas :-
(A) The pipe line and water points along the CAMBRAI Road up to and including TILLOY AREA.
(B) The Battery Valley - FEUCHY CHAPEL Supply.
(C) The RONVILLE - ACHICOURT Area.

The A.P.M. of the Corps will arrange for Military Police to patrol these areas and see that the above orders are carried out.

DIVISIONAL ROUTINE ORDERS
by
Major-General Colin Mackenzie, C.B.,
Commanding 61st Division.
------oOo------

Headquarters, 28th May., 1917.

1164... HONOURS & AWARDS:
Under authority granted by His Majesty The King, (M.S.H. 2260 dated 2-6-16) the G.O.C., IV Corps, has awarded the following decoration:-

MILITARY MEDAL - (Date of award 26-5-1917).

No. 14329, Sgt. R.W. COOK, 183rd M. G. Coy.

1165... ESTIMATED CASUALTIES:
Reference D.R.O. No. 1140 of 14-5-1917 -
The "Estimated Casualty" phase, which commenced midnight 15/16th May will close, and a new phase will open midnight 31st May/1st June.
Any estimates of casualties after the commencement of the new phase will not include those previously submitted.
Each wire will commence with the words "Total Estimated Casualties from 1st June".

1166... GAS APPLIANCES - DEMANDS FOR:
D.R.O. 1069 dated 30-4-1917, is not being complied with.
Unnecessary trouble and delay results if demands for Gas Appliances are sent to the D.A.D.O.S. instead of to the Divisional Gas Officer.

1167... PETROL TINS:
Reference G.R.O. 2212 of 25-5-1917. -
This does not refer to the petrol tins at present carried on the superstructures of water carts.
All units will salvo every petrol tin lying about in the areas they occupy, and return them to O.C. Train at the Divisional Petrol Tin Dump on the WARLUS-DAINVILLE Road, (Map reference L.31.b.5.0., Sheet 51 c.) when sending to draw fuel.
O.C. Train will keep an account of the number returned by each unit.

1168... ARMY FORMS B.213 and F.773.
Reference G.R.O. 2332 dated 24-5-1917. -
(a) Army Forms B.213 made up to and for SATURDAY of each week should be despatched by formations and units in time to reach these Headquarters by 9 a.m. on Sundays.
(b) O.C. 61 Div. Train will, in view of the G.R.O. above mentioned, arrange for A.F's. F.773 to be compiled by Supply Officers from the Strength Column of ration indents (on A.B.55.) dated Saturday of each week.

1169... UNDERCLOTHING - ISSUE OF:
From the date of this order, all issues of underclothing, whether to replace unserviceable or dirty, will be effected by Officer i/c. Divisional Baths, who will utilise his existing stock for this purpose, and indent on the D.A.D.O.S. for what he may require from time to time.
The Officer i/c. Baths will normally only issue underclothing in exchange for similar numbers of unserviceable or dirty articles.
Indents already submitted to the D.A.D.O.S. and which have not been met to date, will hold good, but no further indents for underclothing should be submitted to him unless the Divisional Baths Officer is unable to supply.

P. T. O.

1170... DIVISIONAL SALVAGE OFFICER:- (LOCATION):
The Location of the Divisional Salvage Officer is :-
No. 8, Place de la Prefecture,
ARRAS.

1171... BURIAL RECORD:
VI Corps Routine Order No. 2213 dated 26th May, 1917, is republished for information and guidance :-
The records of all burials in the Corps Area on and after 9th April, 1917, are being registered at Corps Headquarters.
It is particularly requested that any information regarding burials of any officers and other ranks, especially those undertaken by the unit or by friends, in single and isolated graves, should be communicated forwith to this office. This information should always be given if there is any possible doubt of the grave being properly registered. Officers Commanding Units and Chaplains especially should send any information they can on this subject.
This information is at the disposal of all officers and men of units, who should apply through the usual channels. The details required may not always be immediately available, but any enquiries will be attended to as soon as possible. The names of any missing men should be submitted with a view to ascertaining if any have been killed in action. All communications on registration should be earmarked "Burials" and should be sent to Corps Headquarters.
Communications regarding the actual burying will still be sent to the Corps Burial Officer.

This order will be re-published in Brigade and Unit orders.

1172... ARMY AND CORPS ROUTINE ORDERS:
The following Army and Corps Routine Orders are republished as an addendum to Divisional Orders of this date, for information and guidance:-

Third Army Routine Orders:

359; 511; 627; 654; 663; 664; 670; 714; 729;
742; 743; 756; 757.

VI Corps Routine Orders:

1940; 1970; 1972; 1978; 1983; 1988; 1994; 2002;
2003; 2017; 2061; 2075; 2088; 2114; 2116; 2150;
2153; 2169; 2168; 2182.

Bennett
DAA & QMG
Lieut-Colonel,
A.A.&.Q.M.G., 51st Division.

NOTICE:

BATHS:
Officers' Baths are now available in RUE DE L'EGLISE, WARLUS.
Bookings should be made in advance with N.C.O.-in-charge;
Capacity - 2 per half-hour.

EXTRACTS FROM THIRD ARMY AND VI CORPS ROUTINE ORDERS

(REPUBLISHED AS AN ADDENDUM TO 61st DIVISIONAL ROUTINE ORDER No. 1172
dated 28-5-1917.)

HORSES - LOST: (Third Army R.O. No. 359 dated 31-3-1916).
   In order to facilitate the recovery of lost horses or mules, the unit concerned should notify the loss not only to its own Division, but also to its Corps and to the Army, in order that notices may be inserted in Corps and Army Orders.

SANDBAGS - STACKING OF   (Third Army R.O. 511/dated 15-9-16).
   To minimise the risk of fire in stacks of sandbags, the following precautions will be taken :-
   (i)   Stacks will not exceed the following dimensions - 20ft. x 20ft. x 8 ft. high.
   (ii)   Stacks will not be adjacent to the main store. They should be isolated by stacks of iron material, i.e. wire, C.I. sheets, tanks, etc.
   (iii) Stacks will be built on a foundation of stone, chalk, or brick. Wooden sleepers and boards are on no account to be used.
   (iv)   A turnover will be provided for.
   (v)   Fire extinguishing apparatus available will be kept in readiness and an adequate supply of water or sand arranged for.

MECHANICAL TRANSPORT COLUMNS - KNOWLEDGE OF DESTINATION: (Third Army R.O. 627 dated 13-2-17).
   Officers in command of all Horse Drawn or Mechanical Transport Columns will, in future, be held responsible that before starting, the driver of every vehicle in the convoy knows his destination and the route to be followed. Whenever possible, this information is to be given in writing.

TRAFFIC ORDERS: (Third Army R.O. No. 654 dated 5-3-1917).
   Attention is directed to para 29 of Third Army Traffic Orders, which is as follows :-
   "Columns of wheeled transport, guns, lorries, etc., are not to halt in the streets of towns or villages. When it is necessary to halt, the officer or non-commissioned officer in command will see that the rear of the column is clear of the town or village, before giving the order to halt.
   Whenever a block occurs on a road, it is the duty of any officer or non-commissioned officer who may happen to be present, to take steps at once to clear it, and provide a passage for passing vehicles."
This order will be republished in the orders of all units.

IRON RATIONS: (Third Army R.O. No. 663 dated 12-3-1917).
   The Iron Ration is part of every man's fighting equipment. If reinforcements arrive from the base without Iron Rations, investigation should at once be made as to whether Iron Rations were supplied to the men, and, if not, the fact should be reported to Army Headquarters. If, on the other hand, they were irregularly consumed, that is to say, without an order by an officer, disciplinary action will be taken.

GRENADE BOXES: (Third Army R.O. No. 664 dated 12-3-1917).
   Army Routine Order 352 is cancelled.
   All empty grenade boxes should be collected and returned to Ammunition Railheads for return to the base.

PRINTING AND STATIONERY: (Third Army R.O. No. 670 dated 15-3-1917).
   A Field Printing and Stationery Depot has been established for the supply of Regulations, Army Forms, Books, Stationery, Typewriters, etc., to units in the Third Army. Indents for the above stores from units in the Third Army will be addressed in future to :-
       No. 3 Field Printing and Stationery Depot.
   Applications for printing should, however, still be sent to O.C., 3rd Field Survey Coy., R.E., in the first place, in accordance with G.R.O. 1265.

(P. T. O.).

- 2 -

DEAD ANIMALS: (Third Army R.O. No. 714 dated 24-4-17).

When units leave horses or mules dead by the roadside they must report the location of each animal so left to the formation to which they belong.

LIGHTS IN ARRAS: (Third Army R.O. No. 729 dated 1-5-17).

In the town of ARRAS no lights are to be exposed and all windows must be shaded after dark.

PROTECTION OF THE PROPERTY OF THE INHABITANTS IN THE TOWN OF ARRAS: (Third Army R.O. No. 742 dated 8-5-1917).

1. It is necessary that the property of the inhabitants of ARRAS - the majority of whom are compelled to be away from their homes - should be adequately protected, while the town is in occupation of British Troops.

2. Measures have already been taken for the prompt trial of offenders against the person or property of inhabitants, but unless strick police measures are taken regimentally by officers commanding units, immediately billets are taken over, there is great difficulty in apprehending the actual offenders.

3. Every unit on arriving in the town will send its Provost Sergeant to report to the A.P.M. ARRAS, to receive instructions as to the special points to be attended to in policing the area in which the unit is billeted.

On arrival in billets, special regimental police must be told off to examine all doors of closed rooms, to see that they are secure, to report cases where doors of rooms or cupboards have been forced, and to arrest persons attempting to force doors or remove or destroy furniture or other property. Such offenders will be handed over to the A.P.M., ARRAS, for trial by a Field General Court-Martial, convened under Third Army Circular No. 29, dated 5-4-16, by the Town Commandant. The names and units of witnesses will be reported at the same time, with written statements.

4. Officers commanding units will report direct to the Town Commandant, ARRAS, cases in which sealed doors are found forced, and steps will be taken by the latter to have the rooms secured.

5. All troops before entering ARRAS are to be specially warned against theft and destruction; and on arrival the "Orders for Troops in ARRAS" dated 4-4-17, which are posted throughout the town, must be read to all ranks. Officers Commanding units will report to the Town Commandant any billets where more copies of the "Orders for Troops in ARRAS" are required.

6. The Army Commander directs that Commanding Officers exercise strict supervision in these matters in order that there may be no reflection on the conduct of the British Troops occupying ARRAS.

TRAFFIC ORDERS: (Third Army R.O. No. 743 dated 8-5-17).

1. All mounted men will dismount whenever a column halts on the line of march either on account of a block in the traffic or for any other reason, except when the halt is only a momentary one.

2. Whenever mechanical transport, ambulances and motor cars halt on the road, the engines are to be stopped in order to economise petrol. If the halt is likely to be a short one the driver must be ready to start the engine without delay when the transport is able to move on.

The Military Police and Traffic Control personnel will see that these instructions are carried out as in the case of the Traffic Orders, but officers in charge of parties or mechanical transport convoys are in no way relieved of their responsibility for seeing that those orders are obeyed.

(Continued)

CUTTING OF WOOD: (C.R.O. 2002 dated 17-4-17).
Third Army Routine Order No. 705 dated 15-4-17, is republished for information :-
"A.R.O. 653 of 5-3-17 is amended and republished as follows :-
'Damage has been caused to woods and forests in the Third Army area by the indiscriminate cutting of wood by units and individuals, without reference either to the owners or to higher authority.
Wood can only be cut after the necessary arrangements have been made with the owners by the Forest Control Officer, Third Army.
All applications to cut wood for fuel will be referred through Corps and Divisional Headquarters for Corps and Divisional Troops, and through the D.T.S.T. of the Army for Army Troops. Applications to cut wood for Engineer purposes will be referred through C.R.Es. and C.Es. to the Forest Control Officer, Third Army. It is forbidden to cut wood in the Third Army area until application has been made, and sanction received, as above.'

This order will be republished in the orders of all formations and units in the Third Army every month."

SALVAGE: (C.R.O. 2008 dated 21-4-17).
There is considerable want of method in salvage operations. It is noticed that many articles are gathered together and placed in shell holes where they cannot be seen.
All piles of salved articles should be placed in the open in the most conspicuous place possible, and a stick with a piece of rag attached to it stuck in the ground alongside. The piles should be placed as near a track or road as possible.
Any person who knows where collections of unsalved articles are to be found, should acquaint the Corps Salvage Officer, as soon as possible, by means of a telegram sent from the nearest office, or by a direct note.
It is everybody's business to assist in the general scheme of salvage operations.
The above instructions are to be repeated in all Divisional and other orders.

TENTS AND SHELTERS: (C.R.O. 2017 dated 22-4-17).
Under instructions from G.H.Q., the scale of occupation is 14 men to a Tent C.S.L., and 6 men to a Trench Shelter.
Owing to the pressure for tentage, this order is to be strictly adhered to, and all concerned should be notified.
(Authority :- Third Army O/49/7 dated 20-4-17. VI Corps O/66).

BATHS: (C.R.O. 2061 dated 2-5-17).
New Baths have been erected in the Caserne Schramm for the use of troops in Area "A". These baths will be allotted by the Corps Billeting Officer of Area "A". The key of these baths has been handed over to this officer.
The baths in Rue de Lille are for troops in Area "B", and will be allotted by the Corps Billeting Officer of "B" Area.
The officers' baths in Rue des Gaugieres will continue to be administered and allotted by the Sanitary Officer, ARRAS Area.

SALVAGE: (C.R.O. 2075 dated 4-5-17).
Each Division occupying a forward area East of ARRAS, is responsible for salving the copper driving bands off empty shell cases. Chisels and hammers for removing the driving bands can be obtained through the D.A.D.O.S. The copper collected is to be placed in sacks, and delivered to the Ordnance Railhead Officer, at ARRAS.
A weekly report of the amount collected and sent to railhead is to be forwarded to Corps Headquarters by 10 a.m. every Saturday, commencing May 12th. Three or four men working systematically under supervision can collect several hundredweights weekly. This work is not to be neglected on any account

P. T. O.

EMPTY AMMUNITION BOXES - RETURN OF: (C.R.O. 2088 6-5-17).
With reference to the portion of General Routine Order No. 1863 dealing with the return of empty ammunition boxes, fired cartridge cases, etc., the following additional articles should be salved and returned to Ammunition Railhead with "empties" for return to England :-
    Fuze Caps for No. 106 Fuzes;
    Fuze Cylinders;
    4-5" Howitzer Cartridge Case tins, together with rubber covers.
    All transit boxes, including grenade and T.M. component boxes.
    Unused T.M. Cartridges.
    Spare part charges of howitzer cartridges.
    Copper driving bands.
    Unused portions of Howitzer and T.M. Cartridges should as far as possible be returned in M.L. cases.

An amended copy of memorandum, Q.O.S. 13/56/B dated 5-1-17, regarding re-packing of empty cartridge cases, ammunition boxes, etc., can be obtained from Publications Department, Army Printing and Stationery Depot.
(Authority :- Third Army C/36/4, dated 4-5-17. VI Corps Q.1/90.

PETROL TINS: (C.R.O. 2114 dated 10-5-17).
With reference to VI Corps letter No. Q/404 dated 3-5-17, the following is an extract from a sanitary report recently received by this H.Q.:-
"Owing to the fact that so many 2-gallon petrol tins have been left about in the back area, it is noticed at inspections of cookhouses that there is a growing tendency to make use of them as bricks for the construction of fireplaces, ovens, etc.
The heat of the fire melts the solder and renders the tins useless.
It is suggested that the importance of preserving these tins is not sufficiently appreciated by Officers i/c units or their men."
The Corps Commander wishes attention to be once more drawn to this matter, which, it is no exaggeration to say, is one of vital importance.
There is no doubt that regimental officers do not yet in the least realize their responsibilities in this, and in other questions of economy, and it is absolutely necessary that they be made to realize them.
The Corps Commander wishes Divisional and other Commanders to give this their personal attention, and to do all in their power to instil ideas of economy into all ranks.
Administrative Staff Officers should make a point of visiting the billets of units as often as possible, with a view to bringing to light and checking cases of waste. Severe disciplinary measures should be taken in any cases of culpable waste of Government property.
    (VI Corps Q/404).

Continued

- 7 -

BATHS: (C.R.O. 2116 dated 10-5-17).
  (1) The following baths are working in VI Corps Area :-

	Application to be made to:
DUISANS	Camp Commandant, VI Corps.
R.E. Park, DUISANS	C.R.E., VI Corps Troops.
AGNEZ	Town Major.
MONTENESCOURT	-do-
DAINVILLE	-do-
BERNEVILLE	-do-
SIMENCOURT	-do-
ARRAS, Rue de Lille	See C.R.O. 2061.
ARRAS, Schramm Barracks	-do-.

(2) Units are reminded that coal must be delivered at the baths for the number of men bathed. Town Majors in charge of baths will see that this is done, and that sufficient coal is kept to keep the bath running. They will also report at once to "Q", VI Corps, any breakdown or repairs required.

(3) It is hoped to open, within the next few days, clean clothing stores at DUISANS and WARLUS. A notice in Corps Routine Orders will be published as soon as clothing can be drawn at these two places.

(4) A men's bathing place will be open on Saturday, 12th May, at K.11.c.7.6. The water at the deeper end will be eight feet deep.
(VI Corps Q/650).

CAMPING SITES: (C.R.O. 2150 dated 16-5-17).
  Units requiring camping sites in the Corps Area East and South of ARRAS Town are to make enquiries as to vacant areas at the office of the Town Major in the Cambrai Road, ST. SAUVEUR.

The Town Major of ST. SAUVEUR is also in charge of RONVILLE, and can give detailed information as to watering troughs, manure dumps, sanitary arrangements, etc.

There is a separate Town Major for ACHICOURT, and a Sanitary Section in charge of the Corps Areas East of ARRAS.

The Headquarters of this Sanitary Section, 3.a., is Girls' College, Rue du Temple, ST. SAUVEUR.

UNEXPLODED SHELLS: (C.R.O. 2158 dated 17-5-17).
  All unexploded "dud" shells lying about are to be collected and destroyed under Divisional arrangements.

For this purpose, each Division in the line will select a place in the old original German line where shells can be destroyed. This place is to be notified in Divisional Orders and repeated to Corps Headquarters for insertion in Corps Routine Orders. All precautions are to be taken every time any shells are destroyed.

An officer of a Divisional Artillery will be nominated by the Divisions in the line, and this officer will be responsible for collecting the "duds" and bringing them to the selected spot for destruction.

Each Division in the line will detail a special R.E. Officer to destroy the shells.

A weekly report is to be sent in giving a detail of the shells destroyed. First report to be rendered by 10 a.m. on Wednesday 23rd May.
(VI Corps Q/1157).

CORPS HORSE REST STATION: (C.R.O. 2168 dated 18-5-17).
  A Corps Horse Rest Station will open on 21st May, at FAUBOURG D'AMIENS G.26.a.4.4., where horses will be able to obtain grazing and rest.

The following rules are to be observed :-
(a) Applications to send horses to the Rest Station, must be sent to the Officer in charge of the Rest Station, Captain HOBSON, A.V.C., at the above address.
(b) Each horse before admission must be inspected by the A.D.V.S. of the Division and a certificate forwarded certifying freedom from infection or contagious disease.
(c) One man must accompany each five horses sent, and must remain at the Rest Station until the horses have been discharged.
(d) Each horse must be sent with its nose-bag, fly-net, and grooming kit
(e) The total number of horses at the Station is limited to 160.
(VI Corps Q/1160).

- 3 -

UNEXPLODED SHELLS: (C.R.O. 2169 dated 18-5-17).
In continuation of C.R.O. 2158 of 17-5-17, Divisions in the line are also responsible for clearing the town of ARRAS. The dividing line in the town between the two Divisions will be the Rues Baudimont, St. Aubert, Gambetta, inclusive to the left, or Nothern Division, and the areas south of the above will be cleared by the right or Southern Division. Localities where there are shells which require to be removed can be obtained on application to the Town Commandant, ARRAS. The western boundary for clearing purposes in the North and South Line running through the centres of G.20., 26., and 32.
(VI Corps Q/1157).

LIGHT RAILWAYS: (C.R.O. 2182 dated 20-5-17).
The 60 c/m. light railway is now prepared to carry freight of all descriptions under the following conditions : -

(1) Units requiring transport should requisition on -
  (a) Major Carr, S.L.R.O., Third Army, DAINVILLE;
        or
  (b) Lieut. Burge, 31st L.R. (Operating)CO., R.E., "Q" Dump.
Both these officers are on the telephone.
(ii) Requisitions should show : -
  (a) The nature and approximate weight of the freight.
  (b) The map reference of the place the freight is to be taken from.
  (c) The map reference of the place the freight is to be taken to.
  (d) The time at which trucks are required to be placed ready for loading.
  (e) The time at which delivery of the freight is required.
(iii) Requisitions should be placed as early as possible. 12 hours' notice is advisable if delivery is to be ensured.
(iv) Units must provide their own loading and unloading parties.
(v) A guide to accompany the freight is advisable but not necessary if the destination is clearly given.
(vi) The order of priority of stores is as follows : -
  (a) Siege and heavy ammunition.
  (b) Light ammunition.
  (c) R.E. amaterial.
  (d) Rations.
  (e) Empty ammunition boxes, cartridge cases, etc.
  (f) Other stores, such as Ordnance stores, salvage, coal, clean or dirty clothing, etc.
N.B: - Wounded men returning from the front will be given priority over other freights.
(vii) The map references of the sidings now available for loading and off-loading freights will be communicated confidentially to units on application to either of the officers mentioned in para. (i). Loading and off-loading should take place at sidings and not on the main line, but on the more forward part of the system, where there are no sidings, this can be done on the main line.
(VI Corps SQ/314/1).

DIVISIONAL ROUTINE ORDERS,
by
Major-General Colin Mackenzie, C. B.,
Commanding 61st Division.
---------oOo---------

Headquarters, 29th May, 1917.

1173. MACHINE HORSE CLIPPING: STEWART PATTERN: RETURN OF.
In accordance with G.R.O. 2342, all units, with the exception of 2/1st Mobile Veterinary Section, in possession of Machines Horse Clipping, Stewart Pattern, will return them to D.A.D.O.S. immediately.

1174. ANTI-GAS APPLIANCES.
Attention is drawn to the scale of personal Anti-Gas appliances, viz :-

    1 Box Respirator.)
    1 P.H. Helmet.   ) For each officer and man.
    1 pair goggles.   )

The goggles will be carried in a separate compartment in the helmet satchel, and not in the respirator satchel.

N.T. Bennett Capt.
D.A.A.G.
for Lieut-Colonel.
A.A. & Q.M.G.,
61st Division.

NOTICE.

It is proposed to hold an "Old Etonian" dinner on
or   soon after June 4th.
Will all Old Etonians who wish to attend, kindly forward their names to the A.D.C. to G.O.C. Divisional Headquarters, before 2nd June.
The date, time and place, will subsequently be notified to applicants individually.

R.

Number 8.

183 I. M. B.

Support Account Balance Sheets (Duplicate)

June 1916 to June 1917 (Inclusive)

Army Form N. 1531A.
(To be made out in duplicate.)
(In pads of 80.)

FOR USE IN THE FIELD.

ACCOUNT of sums received and expended by the Sub-Accountant during the month of June 1916, in account with the Paymaster i/c Clearing House, Base.

Imprest Account No. Army 1834

183 L.M.B. (Unit.)
(Full official designation of Imprest Holder.)

Dr.

Date	No. of Voucher	From whom received	Particulars	Amount (Local Currency) francs
27.6.16		Field Cashier		350 0

Total Receipts ... ...
Balance due to Paymaster on last Account
Balance due by Paymaster on this Account
TOTAL Dr. 350 0

Cr.

Date	No. of Voucher	To whom paid	Particulars	Amount (Local Currency) francs
27.6.16		Aquitaine Hotel	1-7	225- 0
		Due to Paymaster on close of		125- 0

Total Expenditure ... ...
Balance due by Paymaster on last Account
Balance due to Paymaster on this Account
TOTAL Cr. 350 0

I certify that the above Account is correct.

Station and Date Field 30/6/16 H. Charles Ford Sub-Accountant.

1. This Account is to be made out by the Sub-Accountant (the Vouchers supporting the several credits and charges being annexed and numbered as 'Sub-Vouchers') and should be forwarded as soon after end of month as possible to the Paymaster in charge of Clearing House at the base.
2. When this Form is used by the General Staff in connection with intelligence duties, the Sub-Accountant should attach a Certificate in those cases where it is not possible or expedient to obtain Vouchers.
3. Vouchers or Certificates should be numbered 1, 2, 3, &c., a fresh series of numbers being used for each account.

Army Form N. 1531A.
(To be made out in duplicate.)
(In pads of 50.)

FOR USE IN THE FIELD.

ACCOUNT of sums received and expended by the Sub-Accountant during the month of _July_ 1916, in account with the Paymaster i/c Clearing House, Base.

Imprest Account No. _Army 1894_

183 MLB
(Full official designation of Imprest Holder.) (Unit.)

Dr.

Date	No. of Voucher	From whom received	Particulars	Amount (Local Currency) francs	
7.7.16		Field Cashier		350	0
21.7.16		do		500	0
28.7.16		do		200	0
			Total Receipts		
			Balance due to Paymaster on last Account	125	0
			Balance due by Paymaster on this Account		
			TOTAL Dr.	1075	0

Cr.

Date	No. of Voucher	To whom paid	Particulars	Amount (Local Currency) francs	
14.7.16		Acqu. de Finance Rolls	5 – 8	325	0
21.7.16		do	9 – 12	485	0
28.7.16		do	13 – 16	240	0
			Total Expenditure		
			Balance due by Paymaster on last Account		
			Balance due to Paymaster on this Account	35	0
			TOTAL Cr.	1075	0

I certify that the above Account is correct.

Station and Date _Field 31/7/16_   _[signature]_ Sub-Accountant.

1. This Account is to be made out by the Sub-Accountant (the Vouchers supporting the several credits and charges being annexed and numbered as 'Sub-Vouchers') and should be forwarded as soon after end of month as possible to the Paymaster in charge of Clearing House at the base.
2. When this Form is used by the General Staff in connection with intelligence duties, the Sub-Accountant should attach a Certificate in those cases where it is not possible or expedient to obtain Vouchers.
3. Vouchers or Certificates should be numbered 1, 2, 3, &c., a fresh series of numbers being used for each account.

Army Form N. 1531A.
(To be made out in duplicate.)
(In pads of 50.)

FOR USE IN THE FIELD.

ACCOUNT of sums received and expended by the Sub-Accountant during the month of August 1916, in account with the Paymaster i/c Clearing House, Base.

Imprest Account No. Army 1893

183 Mule (Full official designation of Imprest Holder.) (Unit.)

Dr.

Date	No. of Voucher	From whom received	Particulars	Amount (Local Currency) Francs		
2.8.16		Field Cashier		300	0	
11.8.16		do		400	0	
21.8.16		do		300	0	
31.8.16		do		600	0	
			Total Receipts	35	0	
			Total Dr.	**1635**	**0**	

Balance due to Paymaster on last Account
Balance due by Paymaster on this Account

Cr.

Date	No. of Voucher	To whom paid	Particulars	Amount (Local Currency) Francs	
7.8.16		Acquittance Rolls	17 – 20	300	0
11.8.16		do	21 – 24	263	0
21.8.16		do	25 – 28	423	0
31.8.16		do	29 – 32	452	0
			32 – 38	30	0
			Total Expenditure		
			Balance due by Paymaster on last Account		
			Balance due to Paymaster on this Account	115	0
			Total Cr.	**1635**	**0**

I certify that the above Account is correct.

Station and Date Field 31/8/16 .... Sub-Accountant.

1. This Account is to be made out by the Sub-Accountant (the Vouchers supporting the several credits and charges being annexed and numbered as 'Sub-Vouchers') and should be forwarded as soon after end of month as possible to the Paymaster in charge of Clearing House at the base.
2. When this Form is used by the General Staff in connection with intelligence duties, the Sub-Accountant should attach a Certificate in those cases where it is not possible or expedient to obtain Vouchers.
3. Vouchers or Certificates should be numbered 1, 2, 3, &c., a fresh series of numbers being used for each account.

Army Form N. 1531A.
(To be made out in duplicate.)
(In pads of 50.)

FOR USE IN THE FIELD.

ACCOUNT of sums received and expended by the Sub-Accountant during the month of _September_ 191_6_, in account with the Paymaster i/c Clearing House, Base.

_183 M.U.B._ (Unit.) Imprest Account No. _Army 8xx_
(Full official designation of Imprest Holder.)

Dr.

Date	No. of Voucher	From whom received	Particulars	Amount (Local Currency)
5.9.16		Field Cashier		400 0
12.9.16		"		330 0
19.9.16		"		200 0
26.9.16		"		200 0
			Balance due to Paymaster on last Account	115 0
			Balance due by Paymaster on this Account	5 0
			Total Receipts	
			TOTAL Dr.	1370 0

Cr.

Amount (Local Currency)	Date	No. of Voucher	To whom paid	Particulars	Amount (Local Currency)
	12.9.16		Acquittance Rolls	33–36	740 0
	22.9.16	8	"	39–42	265 0
	30.9.16	9	"	43–46	325 0
				Total Expenditure	
				Balance due by Paymaster on last Account	
				Balance due to Paymaster on this Account	
				TOTAL Cr.	1370 0

I certify that the above Account is correct.

Station and Date _Field 30.9.16_ _M. Charles_ Sub-Accountant.

1. This Account is to be made out by the Sub-Accountant (the Vouchers supporting the several credits and charges being annexed and numbered as 'Sub-Vouchers') and should be forwarded as soon after end of month as possible to the Paymaster in charge of Clearing House at the base.
2. When this Form is used by the General Staff in connection with intelligence duties, the Sub-Accountant should attach a Certificate in those cases where it is not possible or expedient to obtain Vouchers.
3. Vouchers or Certificates should be numbered 1, 2, 3, &c., a fresh series of numbers being used for each account.

Army Form N. 1531A.
(To be made out in duplicate.)
(In pads of 50.)

FOR USE IN THE FIELD.

ACCOUNT of sums received and expended by the Sub-Accountant during the month of _October_ 1916, in account with the Paymaster i/c Clearing House, Base.

Imprest Account No. _Brun Jaya_

_1830 MB_
(Full official designation of Imprest Holder.) (Unit.)

Dr.

Date	No. of Voucher	From whom received	Particulars	Amount (Local Currency)
10.10.16		E.C.		600 0
17.10.16		do		800 0
23.10.16		Field		350 0
			Total Receipts	
			Balance due to Paymaster on last Account	
			Balance due by Paymaster on this Account	
			Total Dr.	1350 0

Cr.

Date	No. of Voucher	To whom paid	Particulars	Amount (Local Currency)
11.10.16	1	Agent Govt Mills	47 — 50	133 0
15.10.16	2			65 0
18.10.16	3	do	51 — 54	350 2
23.10.16	4	do	53 — 58	295 0
27.10.16	5	½ % chu		5
			Total Expenditure	
			Balance due by Paymaster on last Account	
			Balance due to Paymaster on this Account	
			Total Cr.	1350 0

I certify that the above Account is correct.

Station and Date _Field 31/10/16_ _N. Mackay Capt_ Sub-Accountant.

1. This Account is to be made out by the Sub-Accountant (the Vouchers supporting the several credits and charges being annexed and numbered as 'Sub-Vouchers') and should be forwarded as soon after end of month as possible to the Paymaster in charge of Clearing House at the base.
2. When this Form is used by the General Staff in connection with intelligence duties, the Sub-Accountant should attach a Certificate in those cases where it is not possible or expedient to obtain Vouchers.
3. Vouchers or Certificates should be numbered 1, 2, 3, &c., a fresh series of numbers being used for each account.

FOR USE IN THE FIELD.

Army Form N. 1531A.
(To be made out in duplicate.)
(In pads of 50.)

ACCOUNT of sums received and expended by the Sub-Accountant during the month of _October_ 1916, in account with the Paymaster i/c Clearing House, Base.

Gordon B. (Unit.) _183 ???_ Imprest Account No. _?????_
(Full official designation of Imprest Holder.)

Dr.

Date	No. of Voucher	From whom received	Particulars	Amount (Local Currency)
21.10.16		Field Cashier		800 0
			Total Receipts	
			Total Dr.	825 0

Balance due to Paymaster on last Account ...
Balance due by Paymaster on this Account ...

Cr.

Date	No. of Voucher	To whom paid	Particulars	Amount (Local Currency)
31.10.16	1	Acquittance Rolls	59-62	743 0
	2	G. A. Gun		70 0
			Total Expenditure	
		Balance due by Paymaster on last Account		
		Balance due to Paymaster on this Account		
			Total Cr.	813 0

I certify that the above Account is correct.

Station and Date _Field 31/10/16_   _??????_   Sub-Accountant.

1. This Account is to be made out by the Sub-Accountant (the Vouchers supporting the several credits and charges being annexed and numbered as 'Sub-Vouchers') and should be forwarded as soon after end of month as possible to the Paymaster in charge of Clearing House at the base.
2. When this Form is used by the General Staff in connection with intelligence duties, the Sub-Accountant should attach a Certificate in those cases where it is not possible or expedient to obtain Vouchers.
3. Vouchers or Certificates should be numbered 1, 2, 3, &c., a fresh series of numbers being used for each account.

Army Form N. 1531A.
(To be made out in duplicate.)
(In pads of 50.)

FOR USE IN THE FIELD.

ACCOUNT of sums received and expended by the Sub-Accountant during the month of _November_ 191_6_, in account with the Paymaster i/c Clearing House, Base. _183 M.M.B._ (Unit.) Imprest Account No _____

(Full official designation of Imprest Holder.)

Dr.

Date	No. of Voucher	From whom received	Particulars	Amount (Local Currency)
1.11.16		Field Cashier		900 0
12.11.16		Do		300 0
23.11.16		Do		6.00 0
			Total Receipts	
Balance due to Paymaster on last Account				
Balance due by Paymaster on this Account				
			TOTAL Dr.	1,200 0

Cr.

Date	No. of Voucher	To whom paid	Particulars	Amount (Local Currency)
4.11.16		Acquittance Rolls	13-16	183 0
12.11.16	1	R. Bathurst for hire		9 20
		Sundry R. Receipts		
		Captain Thorne for hire		2 0
		Certain A. appearance		25 0
23.11.16		Acquittance Rolls 67-73		572 25
30.11.16		R. Colby Coles		25 2
			Total Expenditure	
			Balance due by Paymaster on last Account	300 0
			Balance due to Paymaster on this Account	
			TOTAL Cr.	1,200 0

I certify that the above Account is correct.

Station and Date _____ _Allinson Capt._ Sub-Accountant.

1. This Account is to be made out by the Sub-Accountant (the Vouchers supporting the several credits and charges being annexed and numbered as 'Sub-Vouchers') and should be forwarded as soon after end of month as possible to the Paymaster in charge of Clearing House at the base.
2. When this Form is used by the General Staff in connection with intelligence duties, the Sub-Accountant should attach a Certificate in those cases where it is not possible or expedient to obtain Vouchers.
3. Vouchers or Certificates should be numbered 1, 2, 3, &c., a fresh series of numbers being used for each account.

Army Form N. 1531A.
(To be made out in duplicate.)
(In pads of 50.)

FOR USE IN THE FIELD.

ACCOUNT of sums received and expended by the Sub-Accountant during the month of _December_ 1916, in account with the Paymaster i/c Clearing House, Base. Imprest Account No _Leave 1894_

_1830 M.I.B._ (Unit.)
(Full official designation of Imprest Holder.)

Dr.

Date	No. of Voucher	From whom received	Particulars	Amount (Local Currency)
1.12.16		Cpl. Cashier	Francs	800 0
		Cpl. Cashier in Rls		5 0
4.12.16		Cpl. Cashier		300 0
		Total Receipts		800 0
			TOTAL Dr.	1663 0

Cr.

Date	No. of Voucher	To whom paid	Particulars	Amount (Local Currency)
			Francs	1030 0
24.12.16		Paymistress Rls	71-45	605 0
23.12.16		do	74-99	13 0
			80	
		Total Expenditure		
		Balance due by Paymaster on last Account		25 0
		Balance due to Paymaster on this Account		
			TOTAL Cr.	1663 0

I certify that the above Account is correct.

Station and Date _Field 1/1/17_ _[signature]_ Sub-Accountant.

1. This Account is to be made out by the Sub-Accountant (the Vouchers supporting the several credits and charges being annexed and numbered as 'Sub-Vouchers') and should be forwarded as soon after end of month as possible to the Paymaster in charge of Clearing House at the base.
2. When this Form is used by the General Staff in connection with intelligence duties, the Sub-Accountant should attach a Certificate in those cases where it is not possible or expedient to obtain Vouchers.
3. Vouchers or Certificates should be numbered 1, 2, 3, &c., a fresh series of numbers being used for each account.

Army Form N. 1581A.
(To be made out in duplicate.)
(In pads of 50.)

FOR USE IN THE FIELD.

ACCOUNT of sums received and expended by the Sub-Accountant during the month of January 191 7, in account with the Paymaster i/c Clearing House, Base.

Imprest Account No. Army 1844

183 MMB
(Full official designation of Imprest Holder.) (Unit.)

Dr.

Date	No. of Voucher	From whom received	Particulars	Amount (Local Currency) Francs
4.1.17	Field Cashier			1000 0
22.1.17	do			1000 0
30.1.17	do			1000 0

Total Receipts

Balance due to Paymaster on last Account ... 25 0
Balance due by Paymaster on this Account ...
TOTAL Dr. 2025 0

Cr.

Date	No. of Voucher	To whom paid	Particulars	Amount (Local Currency) Francs
4.1.17		Argus Force Belg	81-84	745 0
23.1.17		do	85-89	1280 0

Total Expenditure
Balance due by Paymaster on last Account ...
Balance due to Paymaster on this Account ... 1000 0
TOTAL Cr. 2025 0

I certify that the above Account is correct.

Station and Date _____ 31/1/17   _____ Sub-Accountant.

1. This Account is to be made out by the Sub-Accountant (the Vouchers supporting the several credits and charges being annexed and numbered as 'Sub-Vouchers') and should be forwarded as soon after end of month as possible to the Paymaster in charge of Clearing House at the base.
2. When this Form is used by the General Staff in connection with intelligence duties, the Sub-Accountant should attach a Certificate in those cases where it is not possible or expedient to obtain Vouchers.
3. Vouchers or Certificates should be numbered 1, 2, 3, &c., a fresh series of numbers being used for each account.

Army Form N. 1531A.

FOR USE IN THE FIELD.

(To be made out in duplicate.)
(In pads of 50.)

ACCOUNT of sums received and expended by the Sub-Accountant during the month of February 1917, in account with the Paymaster i/c Clearing House, Base. _____ (Unit.) Imprest Account No. Army 1894

_____ 1830/MB
(Full official designation of Imprest Holder.)

Dr.

Date	No. of Voucher	From whom received	Particulars	Amount (Local Currency)
3.2.17		Capt'n Thacker	Repayment of Imprest	
			Sale of advances checked	20 0
10.2.17		Field Casher		600 0
			Total Receipts	1020 0
			Total Dr.	1820 0

Balance due to Paymaster on last Account
Balance due by Paymaster on this Account

Cr.

Date	No. of Voucher	To whom paid	Particulars	Amount (Local Currency)
11.2.17		Acquittance Rolls	89 - 92	1345 0
21.2.17		do	93 - 95	220 0
			Total Expenditure	
			Balance due by Paymaster on last Account	
			Balance due to Paymaster on this Account	255 0
			Total Cr.	1820 0

I certify that the above Account is correct.

Station and Date _____ 28/2/17   _____ Sub-Accountant.

1. This Account is to be made out by the Sub-Accountant (the Vouchers supporting the several credits and charges being annexed and numbered as 'Sub-Vouchers') and should be forwarded as soon after end of month as possible to the Paymaster in charge of Clearing House at the base.
2. When this Form is used by the General Staff in connection with intelligence duties, the Sub-Accountant should attach a Certificate in those cases where it is not possible or expedient to obtain Vouchers.
3. Vouchers or Certificates should be numbered 1, 2, 3, &c., a fresh series of numbers being used for each account.

Army Form N. 1531A.
(To be made out in duplicate.)
(In pads of 50.)

FOR USE IN THE FIELD.

ACCOUNT of sums received and expended by the Sub-Accountant during the month of _March_ 1917, in account with the Paymaster i/c Clearing House, Base.

Unit: _183 M.U.C._
Imprest Account No. _Queen 1943_
(Full official designation of Imprest Holder.)

Dr.

Date	No. of Voucher	From whom received	Particulars	Amount (Local Currency)
			Total Receipts	Francs 253 – 0
			TOTAL Dr.	253 – 0

Balance due to Paymaster on last Account ... ...
Balance due by Paymaster on this Account ... ...

Cr.

Date	No. of Voucher	To whom paid	Particulars	Amount (Local Currency)
	Acquittance	Rolls	96 – 99	Francs 253 – 0
			Total Expenditure	
			Balance due by Paymaster on last Account	
			Balance due to Paymaster on this Account	
			TOTAL Cr.	253 – 0

I certify that the above Account is correct.

[signature], Sub-Accountant.

Station and Date _Field 31/3/17_

1. This Account is to be made out by the Sub-Accountant (the Vouchers supporting the several credits and charges being annexed and numbered as 'Sub-Vouchers') and should be forwarded as soon after end of month as possible to the Paymaster in charge of Clearing House at the base.
2. When this Form is used by the General Staff in connection with intelligence duties, the Sub-Accountant should attach a Certificate in those cases where it is not possible or expedient to obtain Vouchers.
3. Vouchers or Certificates should be numbered 1, 2, 3, &c., a fresh series of numbers being used for each account.

Army Form N. 1531A.
(To be made out in duplicate.)
(In pads of 50.)

FOR USE IN THE FIELD.

ACCOUNT of sums received and expended by the Sub-Accountant during the month of _April_ 191_7_, in account with the Paymaster i/c Clearing House, Base. Imprest Account No. _Anw/894_

183 MIB (Unit.)
(Full official designation of Imprest Holder.)

Dr.

Date	No. of Voucher	From whom received	Particulars	Amount (Local Currency)
12.4.17		Field Cashier		Francs 1000 0
30.4.17		Do		900 0
			Total Receipts	
			TOTAL Dr.	1900 0

Cr.

Date	No. of Voucher	To whom paid	Particulars	Amount (Local Currency)
13.4.17		Agriculture Rolls 100-103		Francs 645 0
22.4.17		Agriculture for Cooker		26 0
23.4.17		Chan - Estra Rolls 104-107		325 0
30.4.17		Acquittance Rolls 108-110		900 0
			Total Expenditure	
		Balance due by Paymaster on last Account		
		Balance due to Paymaster on this Account		4 0
			TOTAL Cr.	1900 0

I certify that the above Account is correct.

Station and Date _Field 30/4/17_ _Mulhausen Capt_ Sub-Accountant.

1. This Account is to be made out by the Sub-Accountant (the Vouchers supporting the several credits and charges being annexed and numbered as 'Sub-Vouchers') and should be forwarded as soon after end of month as possible to the Paymaster in charge of Clearing House at the base.
2. When this Form is used by the General Staff in connection with intelligence duties, the Sub-Accountant should attach a Certificate in those cases where it is not possible or expedient to obtain Vouchers.
3. Vouchers or Certificates should be numbered 1, 2, 3, &c., a fresh series of numbers being used for each account.

Army Form N. 1531A.
(To be made out in duplicate.)
(In pads of 50.)

FOR USE IN THE FIELD.

ACCOUNT of sums received and expended by the Sub-Accountant during the month of _May_ 191_7_, in account with the Paymaster i/c Clearing House, Base.

_183 M.L.B._ (Unit.)
(Full official designation of Imprest Holder)

Imprest Account No _Some byy_

Dr.

Date	No. of Voucher	From whom received	Particulars	Amount (Local Currency)
31.5.17		Paymaster E.C.		Francs 2000 0
		Total Receipts		4 0
			TOTAL Dr.	2004 0

Balance due to Paymaster on last Account
Balance due by Paymaster on this Account

Cr.

Date	No. of Voucher	To whom paid	Particulars	Amount (Local Currency)
24.5.17		Acquittance Roll	111	Francs 100 0
26.5.17		do	112-115	1170 0
29.5.17		do	116-119	243 2
		Total Expenditure		
		Balance due by Paymaster on last Account		
		Balance due to Paymaster on this Account		389 0
			TOTAL Cr.	2004 0

I certify that the above Account is correct.

Station and Date _Field 31/5/17_ _W. Marchese Capt._ Sub-Accountant.

1. This Account is to be made out by the Sub-Accountant (the Vouchers supporting the several credits and charges being annexed and numbered as "Sub-Vouchers") and should be forwarded as soon after end of month as possible to the Paymaster in charge of Clearing House at the base.
2. When this Form is used by the General Staff in connection with intelligence duties, the Sub-Accountant should attach a Certificate in those cases where it is not possible or expedient to obtain Vouchers.
3. Vouchers or Certificates should be numbered 1, 2, 3, &c., a fresh series of numbers being used for each account.

Army Form N. 1531A.
(To be made out in duplicate.)
(In pads of 50.)

FOR USE IN THE FIELD.

ACCOUNT of sums received and expended by the Sub-Accountant during the month of June 1917, in account with the Paymaster i/c Clearing House, Base. 183 MLB (Unit.) Imprest Account No. June 1917

(Full official designation of Imprest Holder.)

Dr.

Date	No. of Voucher	From whom received	Particulars	Amount (Local Currency)
2.6.17		Field Cashier		300 0
13.6.17		do		400 0
20.6.17		do		300 0
26.6.17		do		300 0
			Total Receipts	1289 0
			Balance due to Paymaster on last Account	
			Balance due by Paymaster on this Account	65 0
			Total Dr.	1389 0

Cr.

Date	No. of Voucher	To whom paid	Particulars	Amount (Local Currency)
6.6.17		Acquittance Rolls	120	300 0
9.6.17		do	121-124	325 0
13.6.17		do	125-128	350 0
15.6.17		Imprest Roll	129	5 0
19.6.17		Acquittance Rolls	129-132	220 0
23.6.17		do	133-136	200 0
20.6.17			W1-W3	14 0
27.6.17		do	137-140	390 0
			Total Expenditure	1324 0
			Balance due by Paymaster on last Account	
			Balance due to Paymaster on this Account	65 0
			Total Cr.	1389 0

I certify that the above Account is correct.

Station and Date Field 30.6.17 W.Morton Capt. Sub-Accountant.

I certify that I have in my possession, 65 francs W.M.

1. This Account is to be made out by the Sub-Accountant (the Vouchers supporting the several credits and charges being annexed and numbered as 'Sub-Vouchers') and should be forwarded as soon after end of month as possible to the Paymaster in charge of Clearing House at the base.
2. When this Form is used by the General Staff in connection with intelligence duties, the Sub-Accountant should attach a Certificate in those cases where it is not possible or expedient to obtain Vouchers.
3. Vouchers or Certificates should be numbered 1, 2, 3, &c., a fresh series of numbers being used for each account.

WO 95/30622 (K)

WO 95/30622 (K)

61ST DIVISION
183RD INFY BDE

TRENCH MORTAR BTY
JLY - AUG 1916

Vol III

CONFIDENTIAL

WAR DIARY.

of

183rd Light T.M. Battery.

From 1st July – 31st July 1916

Vol.- 3

Army Form C. 2118.

WAR DIARY
or
INTELLIGENCE SUMMARY.
(Erase heading not required.)

183rd Trench Mortar Battery

Instructions regarding War Diaries and Intelligence Summaries are contained in F. S. Regs., Part II. and the Staff Manual respectively. Title pages will be prepared in manuscript.

Place	Date	Hour	Summary of Events and Information	Remarks and references to Appendices
Fauquissart	1916			
Sector	July 2nd	11.30am	Relieved 184" T.M.B. in line. Guns registered on points N19 a 4.7, N13 c 8.2, N13 b 9.3, N13 a 1.5, N13 c 8.5, N13 c 9.6.5, N13 c 1.6.5, N13 a 9.5.	
do.	July 3. 11pm.		Gr'd twelve rounds for guns on above points.	
do	July 4. 11pm		2" Stokes fired 24 rounds raiding parties raided German trenches.	
do	July 5. 5.30am		Light guns fired on the flanks of raided positions. Fired 250 shells (German gun is driving, found it N.A. accurate)	
do.	July 6. 11.30am		Gr'd enemy occupying German parapet at N19 a 3.7½. 8 shells fired. Moon? Stretcher bearer have been there carrying German.	
do.	July 7. 2 pm.		Fired 5 rounds at sally port with new w.e. observed in enemy parapet.	
do.	July 8. 9.0am		Fourteen fired rifle grenades from N19 a 6½, 9.5. We retaliated with 20 rounds.	
do	July 9. 5 pm.		Fired 10 rounds at N19 a 2, 5, at request of O/C Coy 2/7 Wores. who observed portion of new parapet. No retaliation.	
do	July 13. 1h.		Registered on N19 a 3.7½, 6. Shooting good.	
do	July 19. 10am		Fired forty rounds as registration on F5, F5.9, N13 c 8.2. Shooting g'd.	
do.	July 18. 10am		Registered all 8 guns. In afternoon, I regret guns relieved by 182 Tr M B seemed to require at Dead End Post. at 8.30pm fired with four guns in	

www.ingramcontent.com/pod-product-compliance
Lightning Source LLC
Chambersburg PA
CBHW081440160426
43193CB00013B/2334